# Favorite Folktales and Fabulous Fables

## Reader's Theatre Scripts and Extended Activities for the Primary Classroom

Written and Developed by Lisa Blau

Printed in the United States of America
Published by One From the Heart Educational Resources
14150 NE 20th Street • Suite #223
Bellevue, WA 98007

**ISBN 0-9640333-4-8**

*This book is dedicated to teachers everywhere who wish to instill in their students a love of reading. I applaud all of you.*

Kristen

# Table of Contents

# Favorite Folktales and Fabulous Fables

Dear Readers,

Welcome to the wonderful world of Reader's Theatre! In this book you'll find many of your all-time favorite folktales and fables from around the world in script form ready to share with your students. The exciting scripts and extended activities that you will find in this book will surely enhance your entire program. Folktales and fables are powerful pieces of literature to share with our students because they tell about other places and other times, thereby enhancing both our social studies and multicultural programs. Folktales and fables feature the use of rich and descriptive vocabulary and they serve as ideal models for your students' creative writing endeavors. Folktales and fables have powerful messages such as,

*"good versus evil" and "honesty is a virtue". But most importantly, children simply LOVE folktales and fables.*

*The scripts that you find in this book have been performed many times in my classroom and much of the artwork that you see was created by my students. I am indeed proud of their help in making this book become a reality. As always, my students have always given me great inspiration.*

*Happy Reading to You*
*and Your Students!*
*Lisa Blau*

# Helpful Hints

♥ If you have never used Reader's Theatre, you are in for a real treat! I would suggest starting with one of the shorter and easier scripts such as, "The Lion's Tail". I would also suggest finding a picture book version of the story to share with your students so that the children are familiar with the story.

♥ Be sure to first model what I call, "Reader's Theatre Etiquette". That is, students should speak in a loud, clear voice and use LOTS of enthusiasm. Students should hold their scripts out in front of themselves and avoid covering their faces with the script. To avoid this problem, I just say, "I want to see your beautiful and handsome faces." Whoosh! Down come the scripts! Try it, it works!

♥ Be sure to run off enough scripts so that each student has an individual copy. Members of the listening audience can read along as their classmates perform the scripts. In this way, everyone becomes a part of the learning experience.

♥ Once the script has been performed, have your students rotate parts so that everyone has a chance to be both a reader and a listener. One of the most powerful things that you can do is to become one of the performers, thereby modeling the correct way to read the script. Education is above all the giving of ideas through our actions. And in performing the script along with your students, your actions will speak much louder than your words. Besides, it will be GREAT fun for you and your students!

♥ The beauty of Reader's Theatre is that you can employ any of your favorite pre-reading strategies with the scripts. I often ask students to mark any unfamiliar words so that we can discuss these or add them to our classroom's word banks.

♥ Be sure to honor your students' reading achievements by giving them a certificate found at the back of this book. For added fun, you'll find some masks and Reader's Badges that can easily be reproduced and worn by your students thereby adding a little "something extra" to the reading experience.

# Reader's Badges

- Note - These badges can be used to identify each performer (the readers & characters). They can be run on white paper and students can decorate the badges with felt pens.

# The Lion's Tail

## An African Folktale

A Reader's Theatre Script
Adapted by Lisa Blau

| | | |
|---|---|---|
| Reader #1 | Lion | Hippopotamus |
| Reader #2 | Mouse | Turtle |
| Reader #3 | Monkey | |

Reader #1 - Once upon a time a Lion couldn't find his tail.

Reader #2 - He was very sad.

Reader #3 - A mouse scurried along.

Mouse - Why are you so sad mighty lion?

Reader #2 - The little mouse squeaked.

Lion - I can't find my tail.

Reader #3 - The lion cried.

Mouse - I will look for it for you.

Reader #2 - So the little mouse looked in front of the

lion. The mouse looked behind the lion. But he could not find the lion's tail.

Reader #3 - Then along came a monkey.

Monkey - Why are you so sad mighty lion?

Reader #1 - The monkey asked the lion.

Lion - I can't find my tail.

Monkey - I will help you look for it.

Reader #2 - The monkey looked in front of the lion. The monkey looked behind the lion. He could not find the lion's tail.

Reader #3 - Just then a hippopotamus came crashing through the field.

Hippopotamus - Why are you so sad?

Reader #2 - The hippopotamus asked the lion.

Lion - I can't find my tail.

Reader #1 - The lion cried.

Hippopotamus - I will help you look for it.

Reader #3 - The hippopotamus looked in front of the

lion. The hippopotamus looked behind the lion. He could not find the lion's tail.

Reader #2 - Along came a turtle.

Turtle - Why are you so sad mighty lion?

Lion - I can't find my tail.

Turtle - I'll help you look for it.

Reader #2 - The turtle looked in front of the lion. The turtle looked behind the lion. At last the turtle said to the lion . . .

Turtle - I can find your tail, mighty lion. Please stand up.

Reader #1 - So the lion wiped his tears and stood up.

Reader #2 - And then the turtle said...

Turtle - You couldn't find your tail because you were sitting on it.

Reader #1 - Then the lion said...

Lion - Thank you, friend Turtle. Not only are you very kind, but you are very wise indeed.

All - The End

## ♥ TRIED - AND - TRUE TERRIFIC TEACHING STRATEGIES ♥

- Highlight each reader's script with a highlighter pen to make reading easier for the students.

- While one group reads the script, a second group of students can pantomime the actions of the characters. This is an especially effective strategy for engaging your Chapter I or bilingual students.

- Read! Read! Read! Share the classic book, Andy and the Lion by James Daughtery with your students. This story is divided into three parts. Have your students work in cooperative groups and assign the task of writing a script for each part of the book to your three cooperative groups. Assign the role of "scribe" to one member of each group. The scribe is responsible for writing down the script as his/her group members supply the ideas. Give your students felt pens and large pieces of chart paper to assist them in the initial stages of scripting. Once completed, each group can perform their Reader's Theatre Script for the rest of the class OR invite other classes in to watch as your entire class performs Andy and The Lion...performed in three terrific parts! What fun!

- You can easily adapt this Reader's Theatre script into a complete production for your entire class. Simply add additional animals who will come and ask the lion why he is so sad. Tie this idea into a science unit on African animals by asking students to name animals that live in Africa. In addition, have students describe the way in which each animal moves and the way each animal talks thereby adding a vocabulary lesson to your science unit. Here is a list of ideas that my students came up with:

| Animal Name | How The Animal Moves | How The Animal Talks |
|---|---|---|
| • boa constrictor | • slithered | • hissed |
| • elephant | • thundered | • trumpeted |
| • zebra | • zoomed | • whinnied |
| • hyena | • dashed | • laughed |

- Stage a "Lion's Day" with your class. It's quite simple and LOTS of fun. Just ask students to bring in any books (both fiction and non-fiction) that tell about lions. In addition ask students to also gather any songs or poems about lions to add to your "Lion's Day" celebration.

- One more idea for your "L ion's Day" celebration...have your students read and perform the script, "The Lion's Share"...it's right here in the resourcebook!

- You will find easy-to-make animal headbands for students to wear as they perform the script. Children LOVE these!

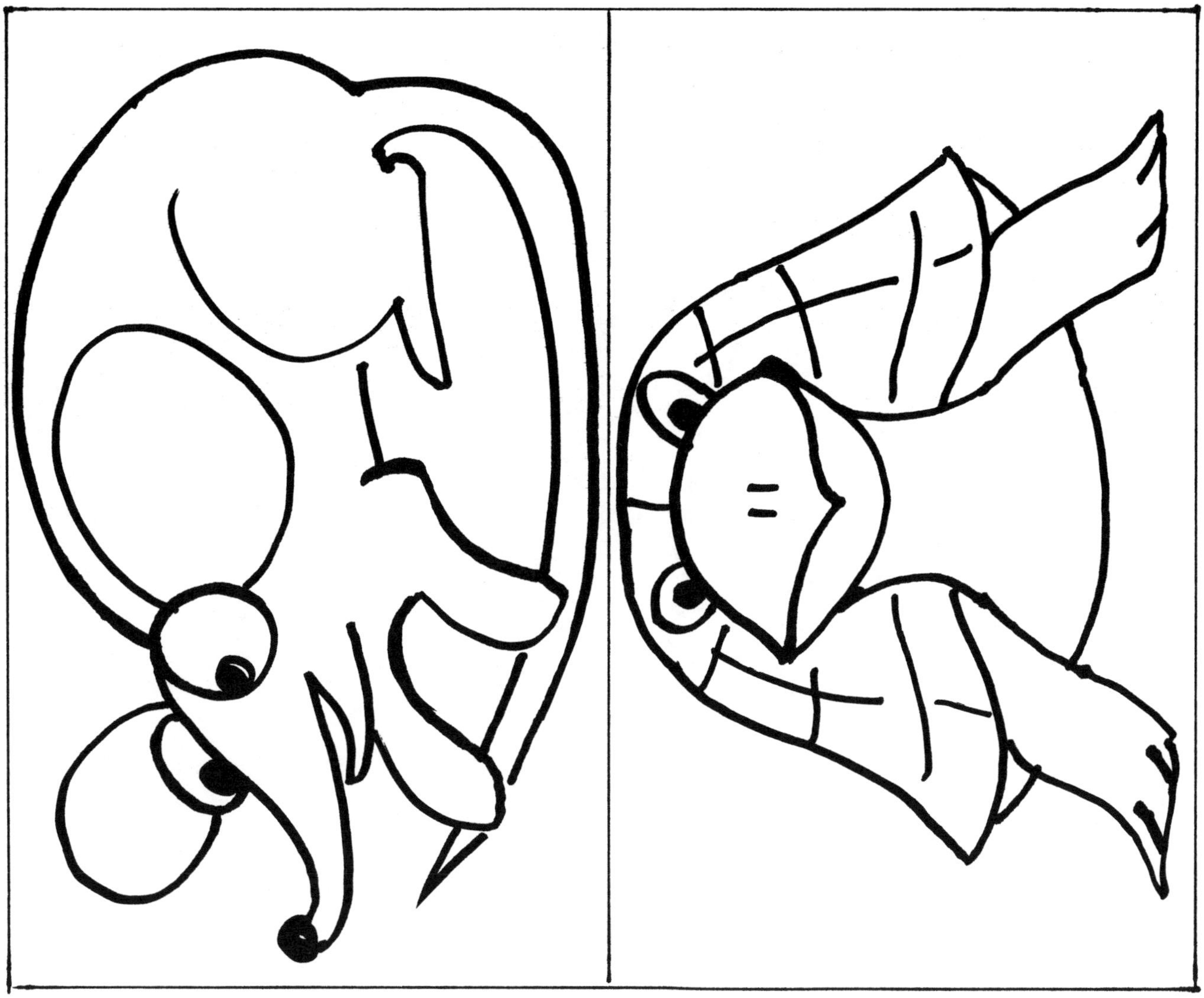

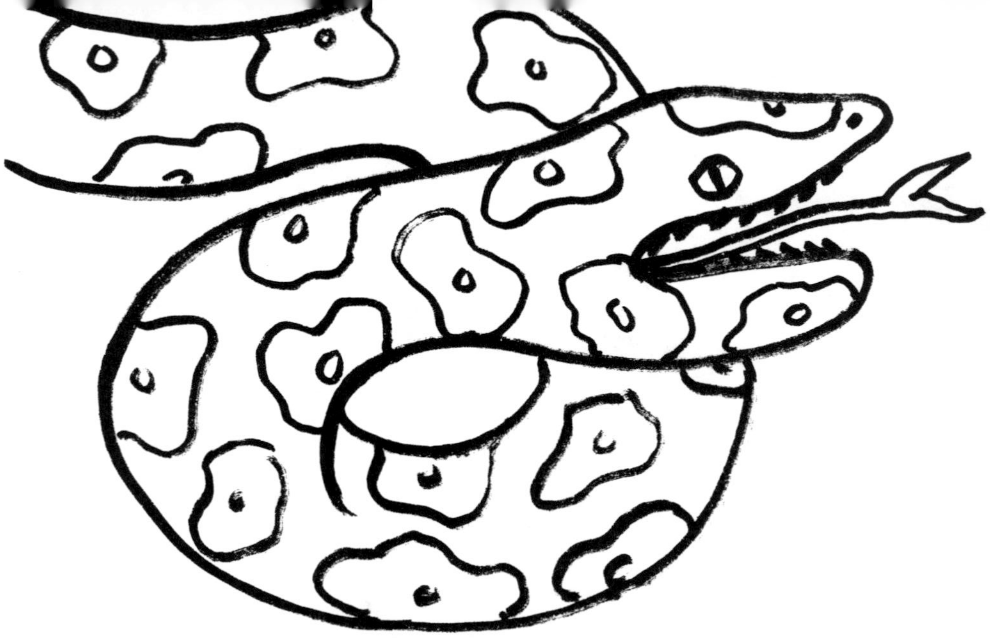

CREATURE HEADBANDS: The students will love coloring these with felt markers. Glue them to brightly colored paper headbands..

# The Stone-Hearted Knight

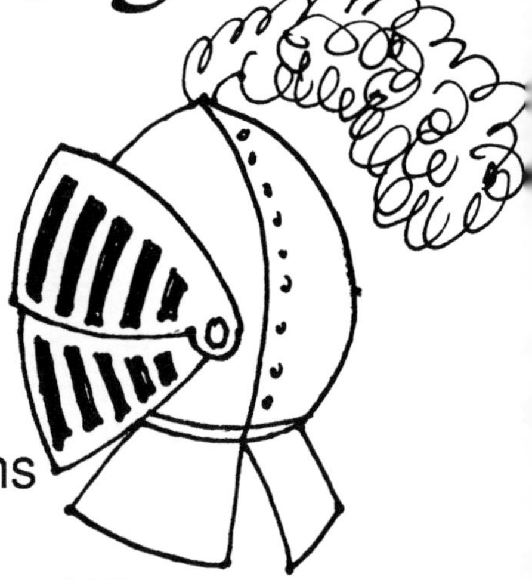

### A Scandinavian Folktale

A Reader's Theatre Script
Adapted by Lisa Blau

| | |
|---|---|
| Storyteller #1 | Young Hans |
| Storyteller #2 | Knight |
| Storyteller #3 | Ingrid, Hans' Wife |

Storyteller #1 - This is a tale of a very greedy and cruel knight.

Storyteller #2 - In fact, this knight was so very mean that people said he had a heart made of stone.

Storyteller #3 - The knight's cruelty filled people with great sadness...but in the end, it was his cruelty that became his own undoing.

Storyteller #1 - As we shall see as we present, "The Stone-Hearted Knight."

Storyteller #2 - Once upon a time a cruel knight ruled the land.

| | |
|---|---|
| Storyteller #1 - | Each day the people in his land had to work very, very hard. They worked from sunrise to sunset. |
| Storyteller #3 - | For all of their hard work, the knight gave the people only a few slices of bread.  |
| Storyteller #2 - | If anyone complained, the mean knight would send them to jail. |
| Storyteller #3 - | Now one day, Poor Hans decided to go see the knight. |
| Storyteller #1 - | He wanted some food for his wife and children. He wanted them to be happy. |
| Storyteller #2 - | So Poor Hans turned to his wife Ingrid and said... |
| Poor Hans - | Today I am going to see our master. I will beg him for more food. |
| Storyteller #1 - | But when his wife heard this news, she began to cry and said... |
| Ingrid - | No! No! No, Hans! You cannot do that. The knight will put you in jail. Please don't go. |

| | |
|---|---|
| Storyteller #3 - | Poor Hans did not like to hear his wife cry, but his family needed more food. He had to go, no matter what. So Poor Hans said... |
| Poor Hans - | Do not worry about me. I will tell the knight about our hungry children. He will give us more food. |
| Storyteller #2 - | So Poor Hans went to the castle of the cruel knight. |
| Storyteller #3 - | The soldiers led Poor Hans to the great dining hall where the knight was gobbling up a huge feast. |
| Storyteller #1 - | An enormous table was filled with all kinds of food...enough food to serve many, many people. |
| Knight - | What goes on here? Who is this man who dares to come to my castle while I am eating my supper? |
| Storyteller #3 - | The cruel knight called out. |
| Poor Hans - | It is I, your grace, Poor Hans. I have come to ask for some food for my family. My children are so very hungry. Please help us. |

Storyteller #2 - Poor Hans said to the knight.

Knight - Guards! Guards! Take this man to jail! He dared to ask me for food! Take him away!

Storyteller #3 - The angry knight roared.

Storyteller #1 - So the guards put Poor Hans in jail. At home, his wife waited for him. Through a tiny window Ingrid watched and waited for Poor Hans to return.

Storyteller #2 - Ingrid spent the night in tears and in the morning they brought her the news that Poor Hans had been thrown in jail.

Storyteller #3 - When she heard this news Ingrid said...

Ingrid - Then I must go to the knight myself. He alone can help me.

Storyteller #1 - Now as Ingrid walked though the woods to the castle, she met the cruel knight who was out for his morning stroll.

Ingrid - My Lord, have pity on me. My husband, Poor Hans is in jail and my children go to sleep hungry. Please help us. Please, sire.

Storyteller #2 - Ingrid said to the knight.

Knight - Ha! Ha! Ha! So, it is food you want! Here, take this stone and feed it to your children. And when it is gone, I shall give you more. Ha! Ha! Ha!

Storyteller #3 - The cruel knight laughed at Ingrid.

Storyteller #1 - Now Ingrid could not bear his cruelty any longer. She took the stone from the knight and held it close to his face.

Storyteller #2 - You beast, how cruel you are! Your heart is cold and hard just like this stone! Oh how I wish I had the power to change you into a cold, hard rock!

Storyteller #1 - Then an amazing thing happened. No sooner had Ingrid spoken these words to the knight, when the knight turned into a cold, hard rock. He had indeed become a lifeless stone.

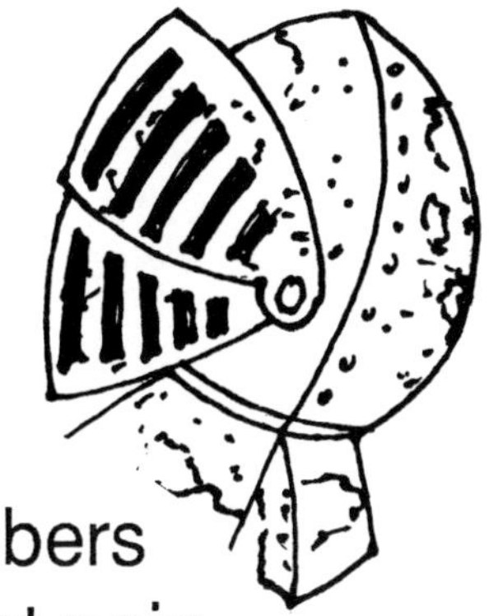

Storyteller #3 - And it is there that he remains to this day.

Storyteller #2 - Everyone who passes by remembers that this cruel knight caused great pain to everyone.

| | |
|---|---|
| Storyteller #1 - | And that in the end, it was the knight's cruelty that changed his life forever. |
| All - | The End |

## ♥ TRIED - AND - TRUE TERRIFIC TEACHING STRATEGIES ♥

- Give your students an opportunity to locate the Scandinavian countries on a map or globe. The beauty of sharing folktales with your students is that in doing so, you'll always have built-in geography and social studies lessons! Encourage students who are of Scandinavian ancestry to bring in any photos or items from home as you learn about this part of the world.

- Read the script through several times so that everyone has a chance to read and to be part of the listening audience. After the script has been performed, engage the students in a discussion about the story. Some possible topics include:

  - What character did you like the most and why?

  - If you lived under the Stone-Hearted Knight's rule, what would you have done?

  - Why do you suppose the knight was so greedy?

  - What does the phrase, "in the end, it was the Knight's cruelty that was his own undoing" mean?

  - What punishment would be best for the knight?

- Encourage your students to look for other folktales that they can script and perform for one another. Join forces with other classes at your school for a "Folktale Festival". Have each class perform a tale from a favorite country.

- Your public library has many excellent folktale books from around the world. Here are some of my favorite titles:

  - *East of the Sun and West of the Moon*
    *21 Norwegian Folktales*
    *by Ingrid and Edgar Parin D'Aulaire*

- *Indian Legends from the Northern Rockies* by Ella E. Clark

Don't miss the multi-volume series by Virginia Haviland:

- *Favorite Tales Told in England*
- *Favorite Tales Told in Germany*
- *Favorite Tales Told in Russia*
- *Favorite Tales Told in Sweden*
- *Favorite Tales Told in Italy*
- *Favorite Tales Told in Spain*
- *Favorite Tales Told in France*

- Say! Is there a storyteller in your community?! Each fall at Back-To-School-Night, I ask parents to let me know if they know of someone (including themselves) who would be willing to come and share folktales from their native land with our class. One year April's grandfather told a spellbound class some folktales from China. Another year, Maria's father told stories from his native Ecuador. The possibilities here are endless and too often we forget about using the members of our school's community as key resources. You may be lucky enough to find several storytellers in your community. What a marvelous way to bridge school and community and to build an awareness and appreciation for other countries. The perfect way to enhance your multicultural program!

- It's time to cook! After sharing folktales from around the world, you may wish to create a cooking lesson featuring easy-to-make ethnic foods. Once again, you may enlist the help of your parents and school community. Edgar's mother helped us make homemade tortillas after sharing folktales from Mexico.

- Cooking in the classroom provides so many exciting and not to mention educational experiences for children. Students are actively engaged in reading and following a recipe's directions, measuring and counting out each ingredient, and learning about nutrition, the science of cooking, and geography. Have students locate each country on a world map as an introduction to your ethnic cooking unit. By sharing ethnic dishes, students can learn an appreciation for other cultures. Storytelling and snacking are a natural pair!

- Looking for easy, kid-tested ethnic recipes to use for your storytelling festival?! Use the marvelous series of children's ethnic cookbooks from Lerner Publication Company. (241 First Avenue, North Minneapolis, Minnesota 55401) Each book features easy-to-follow recipes as well as information regarding special customs related to each recipe.
  The series includes:

  *Cooking the Chinese Way*
  *Cooking the Mexican Way*
  *Cooking the Japanese Way*
  *Cooking the French Way*
  *Cooking the Italian Way*
  *Cooking the Indian Way*
  *Cooking the Spanish Way*
  *Cooking the Norwegian Way*

人

女

# The Story of the One Inch Boy

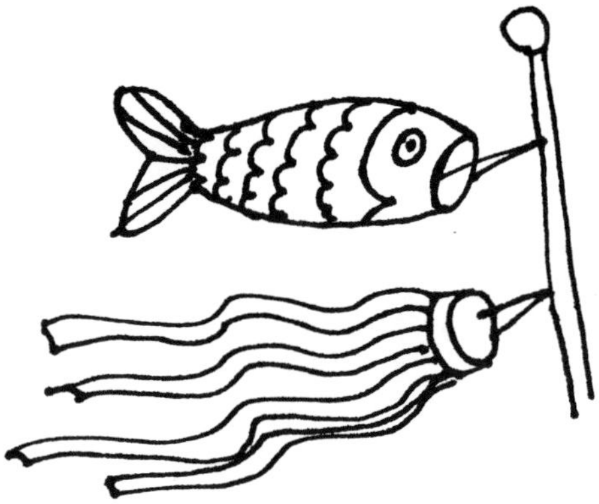

### A Japanese Folktale

A Reader's Theatre Script
Adapted by Lisa Blau

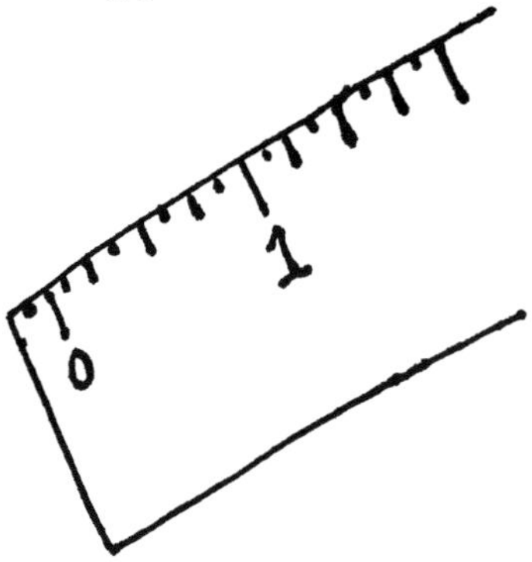


| | | |
|---|---|---|
| Narrator #1 | Old Man | The Lord of Kochi |
| Narrator #2 | Old Woman | The Monster |
| Narrator #3 | One Inch Boy | Princess |

Narrator #1 - Once upon a time there lived an old man and an old woman.

Narrator #2 - They lived in a tiny fishing village in Japan not far from the capital city of Tokyo.

Narrator #3 - The old man and the old woman were happy. But, their lives lacked one thing...

Narrator #2 - The couple wished for a child.

Narrator #1 - Now one afternoon the old man and old woman went to the temple and said...

Old Man - Oh please, give us a child.

Old Woman - We will gladly take any child.

Old Man - Even if it is as small as a thumb. Please grant us our only wish.

Narrator #3 - Not long after this, the old man and the old woman sat looking at the moon.

Narrator #1 - They soon saw something very strange.

Narrator #2 - It was a tiny spot of light coming at them.

Narrator #3 - The spot came nearer and nearer.

Narrator #1 - The spot turned into a tiny cloud that floated into their house.

Narrator #3 - As fast as it came, the strange cloud floated away leaving behind a tiny child.

| | |
|---|---|
| Old Man - | What a miracle! How lucky we are! Our wish has come true! |
| Narrator #1 - | Said the old man. |
| Old Woman - | He is no bigger than a thumb! We shall call him, "One Inch Boy". |
| Narrator #2 - | Said the old woman. |
| Narrator #3 - | Now the years went by quickly, but the tiny child never grew. He was as small as could be. |
| Old Woman - | My husband, our son is so small! He may be crushed as he walks down the street. |
| Narrator #2 - | The old woman said one day. |
| Old Man - | Do not worry, wife. Our son is clever. He can run fast. You need not worry about our One Inch Boy. |
| Narrator #3 - | One day, the One Inch Boy came to his mother and father and said... |
| One Inch Boy - | Oh mother and father...I wish to go to the big city of Kochi and make a name for myself. |

| | |
|---|---|
| Old Man - | And why is that, my son? |
| Narrator #1 - | The Old Man asked. |
| One Inch Boy - | I want you to be proud of me. |
| Narrator #2 - | The One Inch Boy said. |
| Old Man - | Very well, my son. |
| Narrator #3 - | Said the Old Man. |
| Narrator #2 - | Now the Old Man helped the One Inch Boy get ready for his trip. |
| Old Woman - | Our son is too small to sail to Kochi in a boat. What will he do? |
| Narrator #1 - | The Old Woman said. |
| Old Man - | Look here! I have found a boat, an oar, and a sword for our son. |
| Narrator #2 - | Said the Old Man. |

| | |
|---|---|
| Narrator #3 - | The Old Man had a rice bowl for a boat... |
| Narrator #1 - | A chopstick for an oar... |

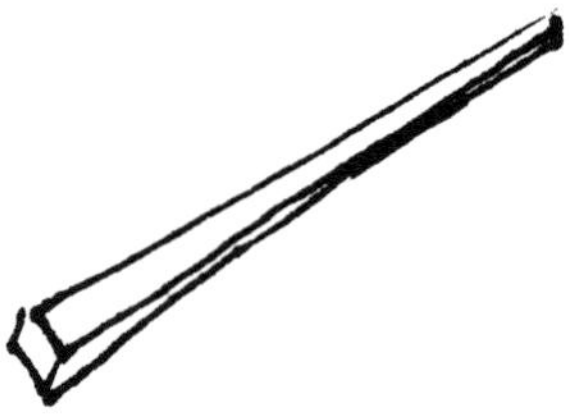

Narrator #3 - And a needle for a sword.

Narrator #2 - He gave these to his son.

Narrator #1 - The next day the One Inch Boy sailed across the sea to Kochi in his tiny rice bowl boat.

One Inch Boy - At last! I am here in the big city of Kochi! I shall visit the great lord and I shall help him!

Narrator #2 - Said the One Inch Boy.

Narrator #3 - So the One Inch Boy walked up to the gate of the Lord of Kochi and said...

One Inch Boy - My Lord of Kochi! I am the One Inch Boy! I am here to help you!

Lord of Kochi - Who is that talking to me? I cannot see you.

Narrator #1 - The Lord of Kochi said.

One Inch Boy - I am down here! I have come to serve you, my lord.

Narrator #3 - The One Inch Boy said.

Lord of Kochi - You tiny fellow! How could you help me?

Narrator #1 - The Lord of Kochi asked.

One Inch Boy - You will find no other like me in all of the world. I am brave and clever! Please let me serve you!

Narrator #2 - The One Inch Boy begged.

Lord of Kochi - Very well, you can be my servant. Here now, polish my shoes and plant a garden for me.

Narrator #1 - The Lord of Kochi said.

Narrator #2 - And the One Inch Boy did each job quickly and perfectly.

Narrator #3 - Now one day a huge monster came to the city. This monster began to tease the Lord's daughter.

One Inch Boy - Here now! Let the princess be!

Narrator #1 - The One Inch Boy called out to the monster.

Monster - Ha! Ha! Ha! What will you do to

me if I do not stop...tiny One Inch Boy?

Narrator #2 - The monster said.

Monster - Do not bother me. Go away or I shall eat you up in one tiny bite!

Narrator #3 - The monster roared.

One Inch Boy - Go ahead...just try!

Narrator #1 - Replied the One Inch Boy.

Narrator #2 - So the monster caught the One Inch Boy and was about to drop the boy into his mouth when all at once...

Narrator #3 - The One Inch Boy hopped up on the monster's nose...

Narrator #1 - And poked the monster with his tiny sword.

Monster - Ouch! Ouch! My eye! My eye!

Narrator #2 - The monster cried out.

Monster - Stop! Stop! I will go away! Please do not hurt me again.

Narrator #3 - Cried the monster.

One Inch Boy - Very well...be off with you!

Narrator #1 - The One Inch Boy said.

Narrator #2 - And as the monster ran away, he dropped his magic hammer.

Princess - Thank you for saving me! How brave you are!

Narrator #1 - The princess said to the One Inch Boy.

Princess - Look here! The monster has left his magic hammer.

Narrator #2 - The princess said.

Princess - You must make a wish...this magic hammer will grant you one wish because you saved me.

Narrator #3 - The princess told the One Inch Boy.

One Inch Boy - Then I wish to be as tall as any man.

Narrator #1 - The One Inch Boy said.

Narrator #2 - And in one second, the One Inch Boy grew and grew and grew until...

Narrator #3 - He was as tall as any man.

One Inch Boy - Now you have helped me!

Narrator #1 - The One Inch Boy smiled at the Princess.

Narrator #2 - And then the One Inch Boy said to the princess...

One Inch Boy - Please marry me, dear princess. I promise to take good care of you.

Princess - Oh yes!

Narrator #3 - Said the princess.

Narrator #1 - And so...the Princess and the One Inch Boy were married and...

All - They lived happily ever after!

## ♥ TRIED - AND - TRUE TERRIFIC TEACHING STRATEGIES ♥

- Help your students locate Japan on a map or globe. Ask students to describe what they see and then explain that Japan is comprised of four main islands and thousands of smaller islands. As a fun geography lesson, your students can draw their own maps of Japan and then show the little Inch Boy's journey from Tokyo to Kochi...and all in a rice bowl for a boat and a chopstick for an oar!

- Visit a local travel agency and ask for any promotional materials such as posters, photos, and brochures about Japan. Travel agencies often have all kinds of marvelous "freebies" for teachers. Such a visit may provide you with many special items to share with your students.

- Read! Read! Read! Be sure to share the following books with your students as they will truly enhance your unit on Japan:

  - Count Your Way Through Japan - by Jim Haskins
  - The One Inch Boy - by Junko Morimoto
  - How my Parents Learned to Eat - by Ina Friedman

- Must Reading!!! Dont' miss Bamboo Hats and a Rice Cake by Ann Tompert (Crown Publishers, 1993). In this wonderful story, the author has incorporated characters from the Japanese alphabet into the text, making the book read much like a rebus story. The illustrations by noted illustrator, Demi are exquisite making this book the perfect addition to your unit on Japan. As an obvious extension, use Tompert's book as a model and ask students to write stories in which they substitute Japanese characters for some of the words in their stories.

- Math! Math! Math! How big is an inch anyway?! The Inch Boy was very small indeed, but students can't always appreciate how tiny an inch can really be. Use the accompanying math worksheet and watch your students make some exciting discoveries about measurement.

- Poetry! Poetry! Poetry! Be sure to read Shel Silverstein's classic poem, "One Inch Tall" to your students. Have students brainstorm the possible advantages to being so small. Students can follow Silverstein's model and create their own poems in honor of the Little One Inch Boy!

- You may also wish to play the Japanese version of "Simon Says". In order to tie it back to the story, we called our game, "The Little Inch Boy Says". The game is played the same way as "Simon Says". The child who is "It" will call out commands and the players must follow. The only difference is that "It" will say, "The Inch Boy Says touch your _______". The body parts will be called out in Japanese:

  nose - hana
  teeth - ha
  mouth - kuchi
  eye - me
  head - atami
  ear - mimi
  neck - kubi
  hair - kami
  hand - te
  fingers - yubi

Name ____________________

# One Inch Math

The little One Inch Boy was very small. Can you find six things in your house that are as small as the One Inch Boy?! Draw a picture in each box to show what you found. Have Fun!

☐ ____________ ☐ ____________ ☐ ____________

☐ ____________ ☐ ____________ ☐ ____________

**Great Fun For Super Star Authors:** Write a story about how you would use these things if you were one inch tall. Use the back of this page and be sure to make a FABULOUS illustration to go with your story!

# Japanese Writing

The Japanese have four ways to write! Kanji (kahn—jee) are Chinese characters made up of different numbers of brush strokes. The characters are written from right to left.

Writing Fun! Use the Kanji below to write a GREAT story. Everytime that you use one of the words below, write the character on your paper. When you are done with your story, give it to a friend to read.

本

BOOK

| 鳥 | 山 | 人 | 川 |
|---|---|---|---|
| BIRD | MOUNTAIN | MAN | RIVER |
| 馬 | 木 | 森 | 魚 |
| HORSE | TREE | FOREST | FISH |

# The Tortoise and the Hare

## A Fable by Aesop

A Reader's Theatre Script
Adapted by Lisa Blau

| | | |
|---|---|---|
| Tortoise | Reader #1 | Raccoon |
| Hare | Reader #2 | Owl |
| Fox | Reader #3 | |

Reader #1 - Good morning! Welcome to our presentation of "The Tortoise and the Hare."

Reader #2 - Our fable was written long, long, ago by a man named Aesop. Aesop always told stories that had a moral at the end. That is, the story could teach the listeners about life and learning.

Reader #3 - As you listen to today's story, why not try to create your own moral. It will be fun!

Hare - Hello! My name is _____________.
I will be reading the part of the Hare.

Tortoise - Greetings! My name is____________. I will be reading the part of the Tortoise today.

Fox - Hello there! My name is ____________.I will be reading the part of the Fox today.

Raccoon - Hello! My name is ______________. I will be reading the part of the Raccoon today.

Owl - My name is ______________. I will be reading the part of the Owl today.

Reader #1 - Our story begins long, long ago in a beautiful forest. The birds were singing, the butterflies were fluttering, and a kind and humble tortoise came walking slowly down the road.

Reader #2 - Just then a fast-talking hare came rushing by. When the hare saw how slowly the tortoise walked he laughed and said...

Hare - Oh, Mr. Tortoise! You move so very slowly. Why I can run circles around the likes of you!

| | |
|---|---|
| Reader #3 - | The hare laughed and laughed at the poor tortoise. At last the kindly tortoise had heard enough of the hare's boasting and bragging. |
| Tortoise - | Let us have a race, my friend. We shall see who is indeed the fastest. |
| Reader #2 - | The tortoise said to the hare. |
| Hare - | Ha! Ha! Ha! A race you say?! Why not?! I'll show you who is the fastest in these woods. I'll win the race, you can be sure of that. |
| Reader #1 - | The boastful hare replied. |
| Reader #2 - | The tortoise said... |
| Tortoise - | The fox will mark off five miles through the woods. The fox shall be the judge. |
| Fox - | I shall be delighted to help my friends. I shall leave at once to mark the course. I will wait for the winner by the edge of the woods. |

| | |
|---|---|
| Reader #3 - | The fox replied. |

Reader #1 - So the fox set off to mark the course. All of the woodland animals gathered to watch the race.

Raccoon - That poor tortoise doesn't stand a chance against that speedy hare. But, just the same, I'd like to see the tortoise win. That boastful, bragging hare needs to learn a lesson or two.

Reader #2 - The raccoon said to the owl.

Owl - My friend, I couldn't agree with you more. We are all tired of the hare's bragging. We will just have to wait and see what happens.

Reader #3 - Replied the Owl.

Reader #1 - The animals lined up at the starting line. Then Raccoon and Owl both said...

Raccoon and Owl - Runners take your mark! Get set...GO!!!

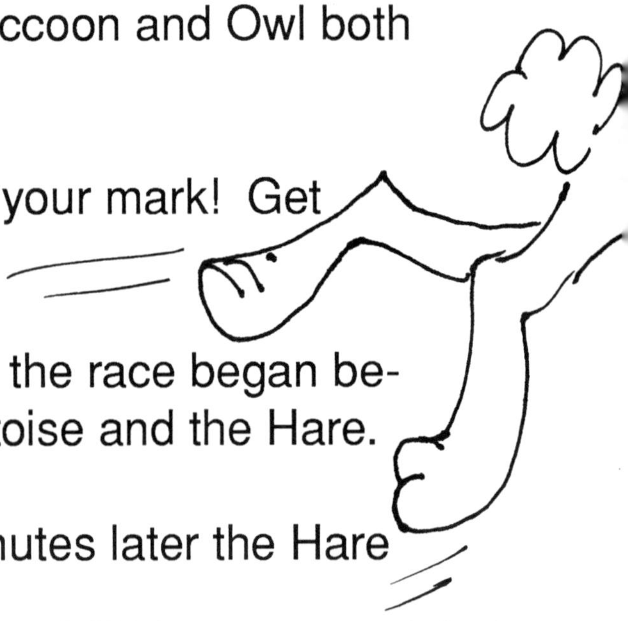

Reader #2 - And with that, the race began between the Tortoise and the Hare.

Reader #1 - About five minutes later the Hare said...

| | |
|---|---|
| Hare - | Ha! Ha! Ha! That Tortoise is still back at the starting gate. He'll never be faster than me! I think I'll just sit under this fine oak tree and take a nap before finishing the race. That slow old Tortoise will still be far behind a fast runner like me! |
| Reader #3 - | So the Hare fell asleep while the Tortoise continued the race at his slow and steady pace. Though the course was long and the sun was hot, the Tortoise never gave up. |
| Reader #1 - | The boastful Hare overslept and got to the finish line well behind the Tortoise. |
| Hare - | I cannot believe that I lost the race to the likes of you. I just can't believe it! |
| Reader #2 - | Said the Hare. |
| Reader #3 - | The Tortoise smiled and said... |
| Tortoise - | A slow and steady pace was all it took to win this race. |
| All - | The End! |

## ♥ TRIED - AND - TRUE TERRIFIC TEACHING STRATEGIES ♥

- As a pre-reading activity you can give the following instructions to your students "I want you to be detectives...word detectives, that is!!! I want you to look for any new or unfamiliar words. Look for interesting describing words. If you find some of these words, write them on the back of your script." After allowing the students...er...detectives...to read through the script in search of new or unfamiliar words, ask students what they came up with. No fair saying, "I couldn't find any." EVERYONE has to find at least one word. List the student responses on the board. Find these words as they appear in the script. Ask students to define these words by using context clues. A great vocabulary lesson where everyone is actively engaged!

- One word my students all found was boastful. This word was used to describe the Hare. You can ask students to think of other words to describe the Hare, then do the same with the Tortoise. OR use the accompanying chart for an activity that students really enjoy. Ask students to think of other characters who share the Hare's qualities. What happened to these other boastful characters?! Many of my students compared the boastful Hare to Loudmouth George from several books by Nancy Carlson. Chart pages can be given to partners or cooperative group members who will report their findings to the entire class. For a slight twist to this activity, some class members could look for other storybook characters who share the Tortoise's qualities of determination and persistence.

- Masks! Masks! Masks! You will find masks that your students can color and then wear to add to your performance. The masks are very easy to make. Simply provide students with xerox copies of the masks, then allow time for students to color in the masks. Felt pens work best of all - the bright colors are more visually appealing to the audience. Instruct your students to cut out the masks and staple onto sentence strips. The narrators can wear badges identifying themselves. Simply use double-sided tape to attach these to the children's clothing. And here's an added helpful hint - run these badges on Astrobright Paper, then laminate so that the badges can be used throughout the school year. Your students will love these!

# Terrific Totems for Fabulous Fables!:

- Children will enjoy making "fable totems" as a way to remember their favorite fable by Aesop. Provide students with stiff Kraft Paper that measures the size of a Pringles brand potato chip canister. Have students draw scenes from their favorite fables onto the Kraft Paper, then tape the paper to the canister. What's inside the canister you ask?!!! Potato chips?! Certainly not! Have groups of students work together to write their own reader's theatre scripts based on any of Aesop's Fables! Your students will have a lasting way to remember this special unit of study as well as a handy way to carry home the reader's theatre script to perform for family and friends...give this as a homework assignment. Kids <u>love</u> performing the scripts and they will be reading, reading, and <u>READING</u>!!! Best of all, this homework assignment only requires a parent's signature and for your part...no correcting! Simple...but <u>effective</u>.

- A visit to the library will net you a variety of Aesop's fables retold by some of today's favorite authors and illustrators. Encourage your students to look for fables either at home or at the public library. Be sure to look for some of these outstanding books to share with your students:

- <u>Anno's Aesop</u> - retold and illustrated by Mitsumasa Anno
- <u>Aesop's Fables</u> - illustrated by Arthur Rackham
- <u>Three Aesop Fox Fables</u> - retold and illustrated by Paul Galdone
- <u>Aesop's Fables</u> - illustrated by Fulvio Testa
- <u>Once in a Wood-Ten Tales from Aesop</u> - adapted and illustrated by Eve Rice
- <u>Aesop's Fables</u> - retold and illustrated by Heidi Holder

- After reading several versions of the same fable, have students discuss any similarities or differences. It is also rewarding to have students compare the illustrations from each of the books. Build the visual literacy skills of your students by having the students discuss the similarities or differences between each book's illustrations. For example, Arthur Rackham's drawings are dark and somber, while Paul Galdone's pencil and watercolor drawings have a more whimsical quality. It is interesting to have students not only share their ideas, but to choose the illustrations that they like the best.

# CHARACTER COMPARISONS

These characters were all: ________________

| Character's Name | Story/Author | Describe one or two events that tell about the character | Consequences of the character's Words or Actions |
|---|---|---|---|
| | | | |
| | | | |
| | | | |

RACCOON MASK

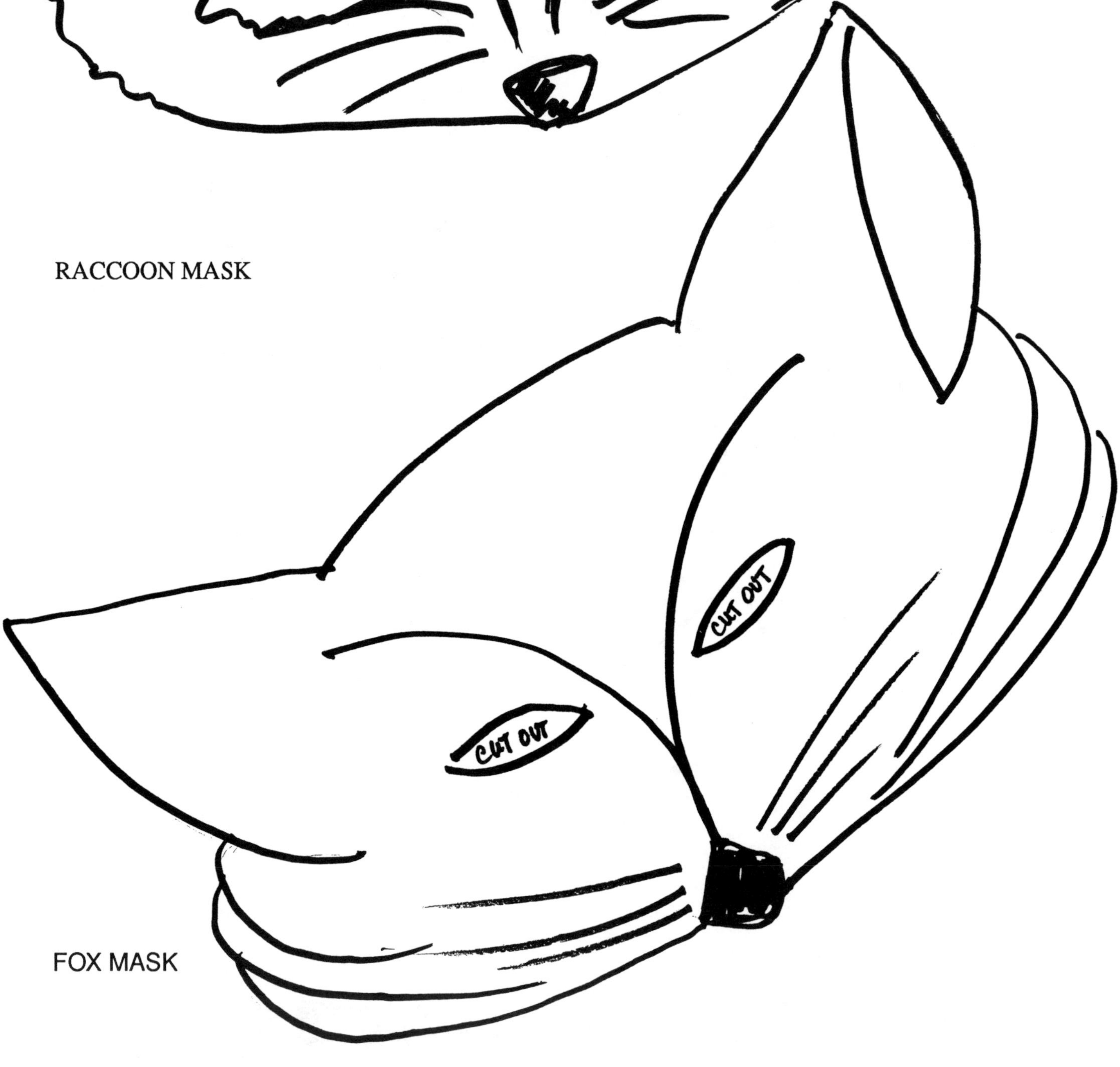


FOX MASK

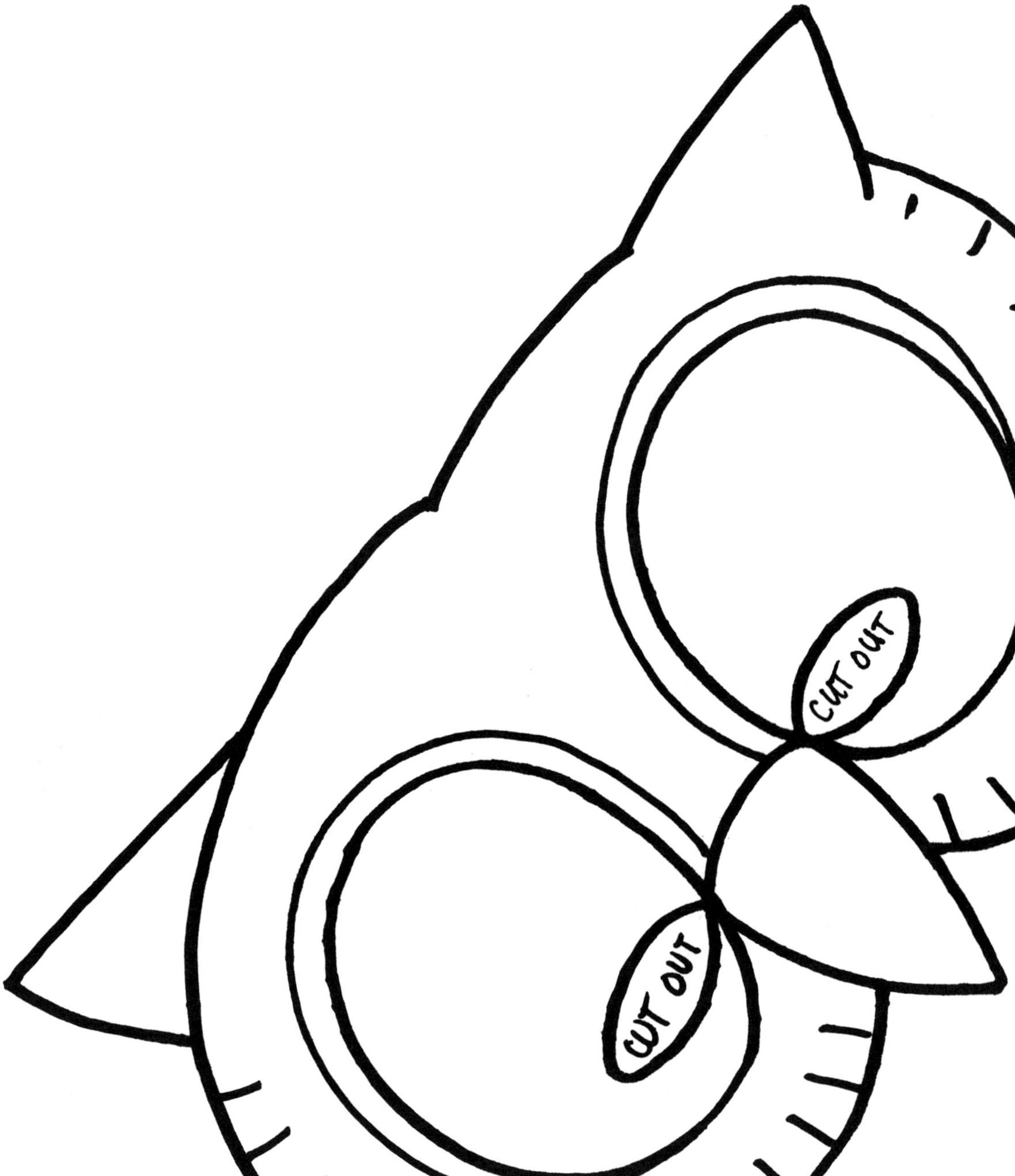


OWL MASK

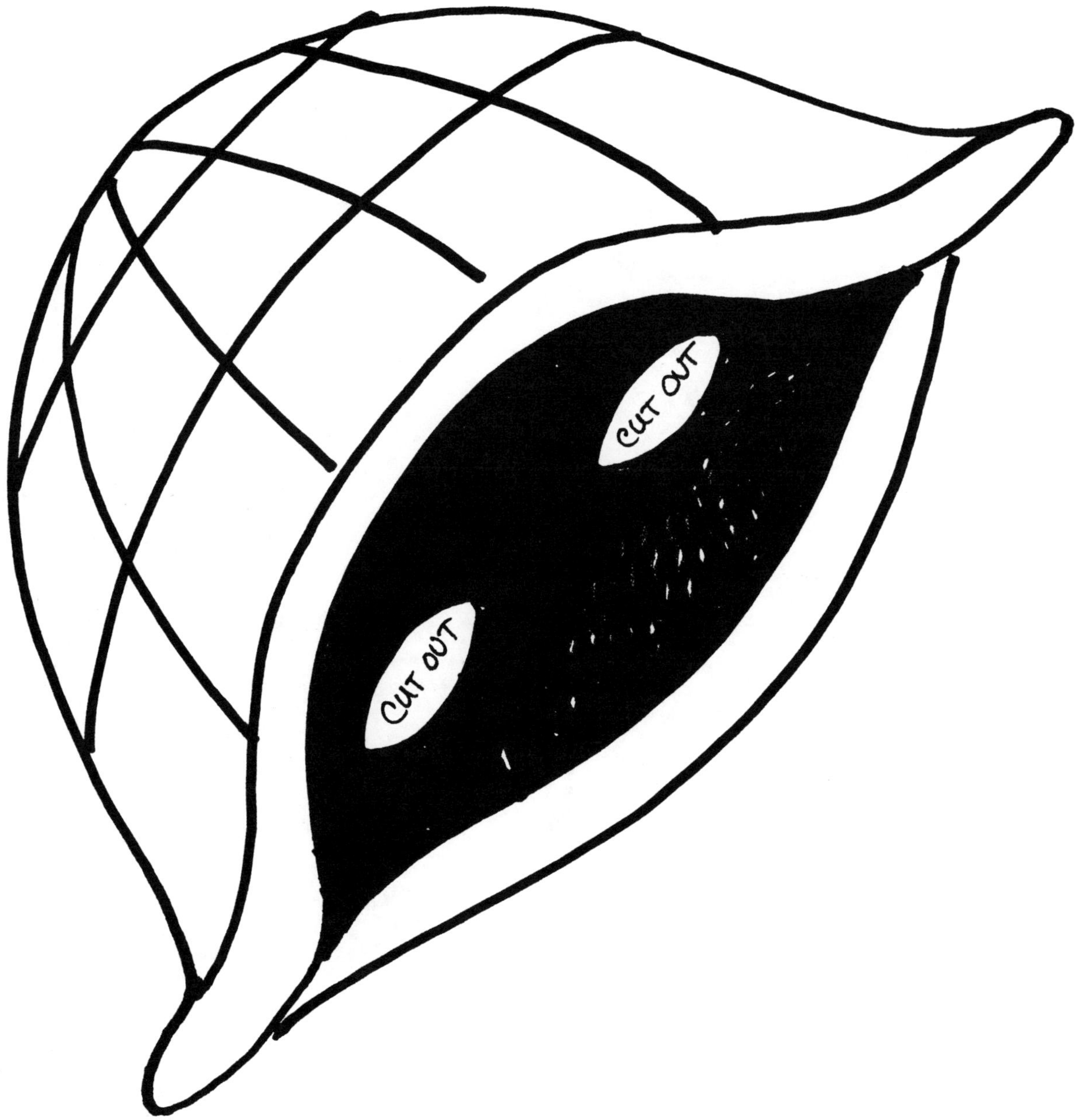


TORTOISE MASK

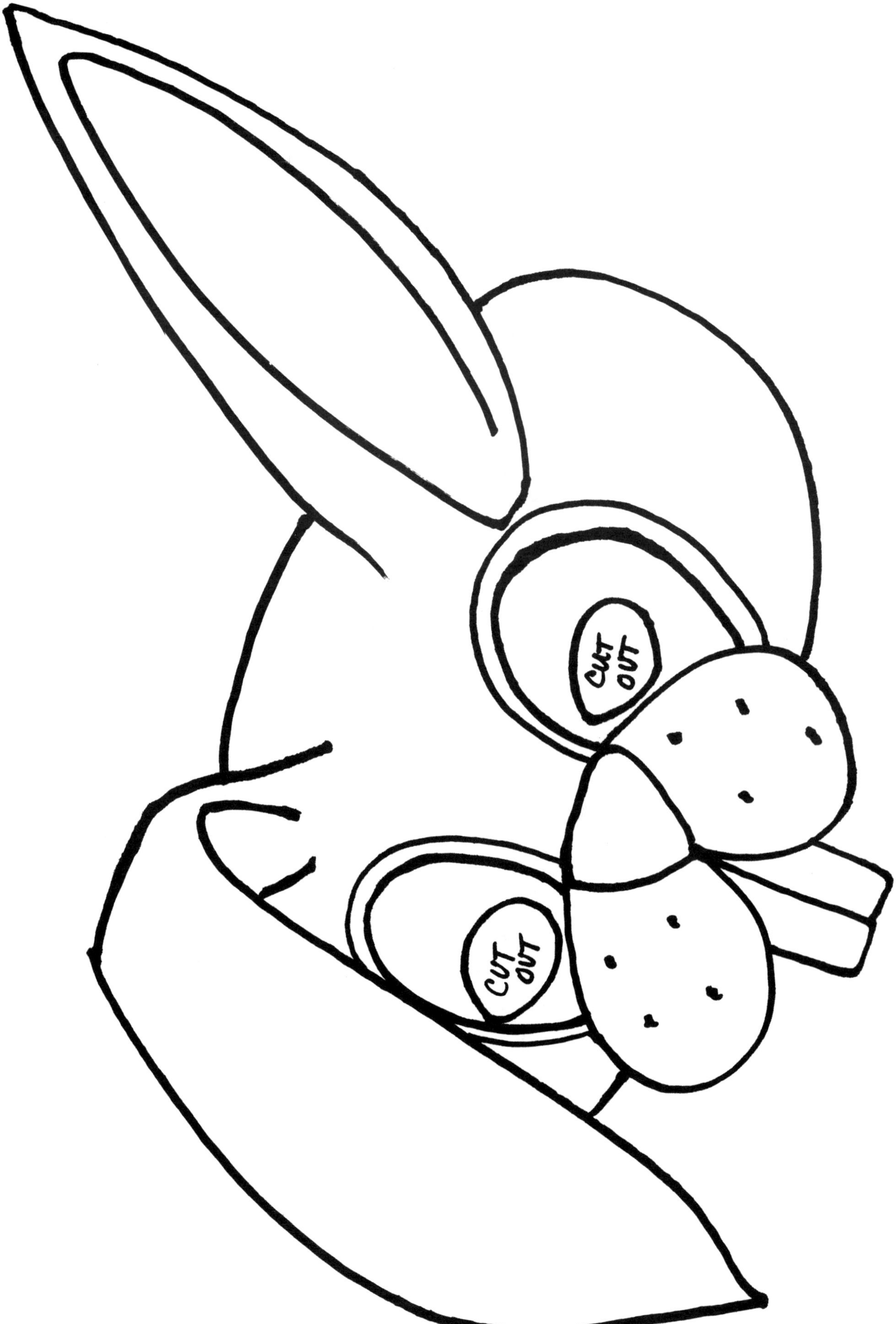


HARE MASK

# The Princess and the Pea

## A Story by Hans Christian Andersen

A Reader's Theatre Script
Adapted by Lisa Blau

| | | |
|---|---|---|
| Storyteller #1 | Princess | King |
| Storyteller #2 | Queen | |
| Storyteller #3 | Chambermaid | |

Storyteller #1 - Good morning! We're here to tell you all a most wonderful story called...

All - The Princess and the Pea.

Storyteller #3 - Our story was written by Hans Christian Andersen.

Storyteller #2 - Our story begins long ago in a faraway land.

Storyteller #3 - A king and queen wanted their son the prince to marry a beautiful princess.

Queen - Alas! Our son the prince must find himself a beautiful princess.

Storyteller #2 - The queen said to the king one fine day.

King - Yes, yes. I agree. Our son should find himself a bride.

Storyteller #3 - The king replied.

Queen - Our son must marry a real princess. One that moves with beauty and grace. A real princess . . . yes, that's what we need for our son.

King- Where will we ever find a real princess? How will we be able to tell her apart from all of the other fair maidens in our kingdom?

Storyteller #2 - The king asked the queen.

Queen - Let us send out a royal proclamation. We shall invite all of the maidens in the kingdoms to the palace. We shall find a princess for our son.

King - A brilliant idea, my dear!

Storyteller #1 - So a royal proclamation was sent out across the land.

Storyteller #3 - And on the appointed day, all of the fair maidens came to the palace in hopes of becoming the prince's bride.

Queen - Alas! Not one of these maidens will do. We need a <u>real</u> princess.

Storyteller #2 - The queen lamented.

Storyteller #1 - Late that night, during a heavy rain, a young maiden knocked upon the palace door.

Storyteller #2 - The chambermaid opened the huge door.

Princess - Please, please, kind chambermaid. May I come in? I am so very cold.

Storyteller #3 - The maiden said to the chambermaid.

Storyteller #2 - So the chambermaid let the bedraggled princess enter the castle. Then the chambermaid said . . .

Chambermaid - Wait here. I shall tell the queen of your arrival. She will want to see you.

Storyteller #1 - So the chambermaid left to tell the queen of the young stranger who had been caught in the storm.

Storyteller #2 - A few moments later the queen arrived and said to the princess . . .

Queen - Goodness gracious! What a sight you are! Why, you are soaked to the bone! Tell me my dear, what is your name and where did you come from?

Princess - I am Princess (add student's name). I live in a neighboring kingdom, but I became lost in the storm.

Storyteller #3 - The princess said to the queen.

Queen - A princess, you say? Well, come with me my dear. We shall give you a warm bath, dry clothes, and a soft feather bed to sleep in.

Storyteller #3 - Now as Princess (add student's name) prepared for her bath, the queen said to her chambermaid . . .

Queen - A princess, indeed! She looks more like a drowned rat! Quickly! Fetch me a tiny pea from the garden.

Chambermaid - Yes, my lady. What will we do with the tiny pea from the royal garden?

Storyteller #1 - The chambermaid asked the queen.

Queen - We shall place it under a pile of twenty

mattresses. If our princess slumbers peacefully, we will know that she is not a real princess.

Storyteller #3 - The chambermaid returned with the pea and placed it under a pile of twenty mattresses. The queen watched the princess and smiled.

Storyteller #1 - The princess climbed on top of the mattresses and said to the queen . . .

Princess - Good night, my lady. I thank you for your kindness.

Queen - Yes, yes, my dear. Sleep well.

Chambermaid - Pleasant dreams, fair princess.

Storyteller #2 - In the morning, the queen hurried to Princess (student's name) chambers. She wanted to know if the princess had fallen asleep.

Storyteller #1 - For if the beautiful princess had not slumbered . . . the queen would know that she was indeed a real princess.

Queen - Good morning, my dear! How did you sleep?!

| | |
|---|---|
| Storyteller #2 - | The queen asked the princess. |
| Princess - | Alas, my lady. I did not sleep a wink. I tossed and turned the whole night. |
| Storyteller #3 - | The princess told the queen. |
| Queen - | Really? Well, well . . . this is big news! |
| Chambermaid - | Our young princess did not fall asleep. She is indeed a real princess. |
| Queen - | Yes, yes. She is a real princess and will be the perfect bride for the prince. |
| Storyteller #1 - | So the prince and princess were married and they lived happily ever after. |
| Storyteller #2 - | And as for the tiny pea that had been placed under the many mattresses . . . well . . . |
| Queen - | Oh that! We put it in a museum for everyone to see. |
| Princess - | And that is where it remains to this very day. |
| All - | The End. |

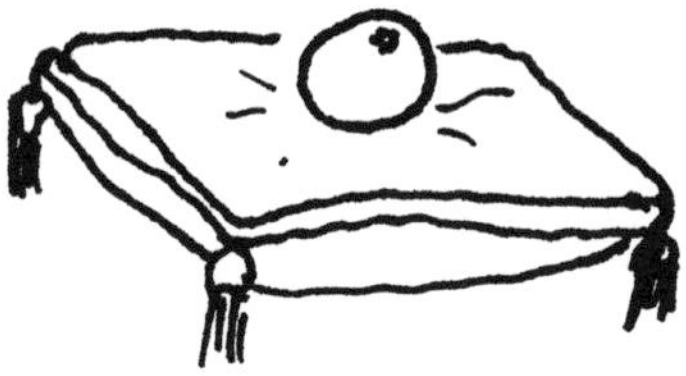

## ♥ TRIED - AND - TRUE TERRIFIC TEACHING STRATEGIES ♥

- Highlight each reader's script for easier reading and be sure to have the girl who reads that part of the princess add her name to the script as needed.

- There are many words in the script that may be new or unfamiliar to your students. Review the script as a pre-reading activity and list these words on the board. Your list may include:

    - bedraggled
    - replied
    - proclamation
    - chambermaid
    - appointed
    - prepared

- Encourage your students to define the above words by carefully checking each word as it appears in the text. Guide students to each word's meaning through context clues. Ask students to try to use each of the words in a new sentence.

- Geography! Geography! Geography! Hans Christian Andersen lived in Denmark. Ask students to locate Denmark on a map or globe. Have a small group of students do some "research" about Denmark and Hans Christian Andersen by looking up these topics in an encyclopedia - a great cooperative group activity! Group members can report on the information to the entire class. Students can also write the research information in their journals or reading logs.

- Your students will find Hans Christian Andersen to be a very interesting author. Andersen was born in Denmark on April 2, 1805. His family was very poor. His father was a shoemaker who would often read stories to a young Hans each evening. At the age of 11, Hans' father had died, leaving Hans alone and sad. Hans left school at the age of 14 to work in a cloth mill. He was very tall and clumsy. Hans dreamed of becoming a singer, dancer, or actor. He went back to school at the age of 17 and began writing folktales. Soon his tales were heard in many countries. Hans was invited to visit kings and queens. It has been said that Anderson wrote the story of "The Ugly Duckling" about himself.

One of Andersen's most famous stories is "The Little Mermaid". A statue of the Little Mermaid sitting on a rock is in Copenhagen harbor. It reminds the people of Denmark of their very talented author, Hans Christian Andersen.

- Read! Read! Read! Be sure to share a most wonderful collection of tales by Hans Christian Andersen entitled, Seven Tales by H.C. Andersen by Eva Le Gallienne (Harper and Row Publishers. ISBN#0-06-443172-X). The text is easy enough for most young students and the delightful illustrations by Maurice Sendak make this a truly delightful addition to any teacher's or school library collection. After reading such Andersen classics as The Steadfast Tin Soldier or The Ugly Duckling, you can have students write their own reader's theatre scripts.

- To script stories as a class project is very easy and lots of fun. After reading the story, have students retell the story in their own words. Next, using large pieces of chart paper, have students discuss the possible flow of dialogue between characters. Sometimes inviting students to the front of the room to try out the dialogue works well in determining any changes that you may wish to make. A final copy of the script can be printed onto the computer. Here's one helpful hint: Ask a parent who may work as a secretary if they would be willing to type up scripts at home for you. Sometimes working parents are delighted to help out in this way.

- Host a salute to Hans Christian Andersen!!! Send invitations to other classes and have your class perform several of Andersen's most famous stories. Entry tickets for guests can be copied below.

## Cooks in the Classroom!

- Looking for a tasty treat to serve your guests after the performance? Try the Danish Butter Cookie recipe...it's fast, it's fun, it's FABULOUS!!!

**Danish Butter Cookies**

1/2 c. butter
2/3 cup granulated sugar
2 eggs
1 tsp. vanilla
2 1/2 c. flour
2 tsp. baking powder

**Directions:** Cream butter and sugar, add eggs and vanilla. Sift flour and baking powder, stir into mixture. Refrigerate one hour. Roll chilled dough onto lightly floured board. Cut dough into desired shapes - create Andersen character cut-outs...ducks and tins soldiers?!! Sprinkle sugar over cut-out cookies. Place on greased cookie sheet. Bake 8-10 minutes. Cool on a rack. Serve to guests after performing scripts!

# *El Cabrito y Los Chiles...*
# *The Billy Goat and the Chiles*

*A Mexican Folktale*

A Reader's Theatre Script
Adapted by Lisa Blau

| | | |
|---|---|---|
| Storyteller #1 | Farmer | Cat |
| Storyteller #2 | Farmer's Wife | Bull |
| Storyteller #3 | Rooster | Little Red Ant |
| Billy Goat | Dog | |

Storyteller #1 - Hello and welcome friends! We have a very special treat for you. We will share a story from Mexico called...

All - El Cabrito y Los Chiles.

Storyteller #3 - Or in other words...The Billy Goat and the Chiles.

Storyteller #2 - Our story begins on a bright sunny day. A farmer and his wife were working very hard in their vegetable garden.

Storyteller #1 - A Billy Goat walked into the garden and began to eat all of their beautiful chiles.

| | |
|---|---|
| Farmer - | Get out! Get out! Get out of our garden! |
| Farmer's Wife - | Stop eating our chiles, you naughty Billy Goat! |
| Storyteller #1 - | The farmer and his wife shouted at the Billy Goat. Then the Billy Goat laughed and said... |
| Billy Goat - | Ha! Ha! Ha! No! No! No! |
| Storyteller #3 - | So, the farmer and his wife called their rooster... |

| | |
|---|---|
| Farmer - | Rooster, Rooster! Help us get that Billy Goat out of our garden! |
| Farmer's Wife - | Make him stop eating our chiles! |
| Storyteller #2 - | So, the rooster squawked at the Billy Goat... |
| Rooster - | Billy Goat, naughty old Billy Goat, get out of our garden and stop eating our chiles! |
| Storyteller #3 - | And the Billy Goat just laughed at the rooster and said... |
| Billy Goat - | Ha! Ha! Ha! No! No! No! |

| | |
|---|---|
| Storyteller #2 - | And the Billy Goat flipped the rooster into the air. |
| Storyteller #1 - | So, the farmer and his wife called their cat... |
| Farmer - | Cat, Cat! Help us get that Billy Goat out of our garden! |
| Farmer's Wife - | Make him stop eating our chiles! |
| Storyteller #2 - | So, the cat meowed at the Billy Goat... |
| Cat - | Billy Goat, naughty Billy Goat...get out of our garden and stop eating our chiles! |
| Storyteller #1 - | And the Billy Goat laughed and said... |
| Billy Goat - | Ha! Ha! Ha! No! No! No! |
| Storyteller #2 - | And the Billy Goat flipped the cat into the air. |
| Storyteller #3 - | So, the farmer and his wife called their dog... |
| Farmer - | Dog, Dog! Help us get that Billy Goat out of our garden! |
| Farmer's Wife - | Make him stop eating our chiles! |

| | |
|---|---|
| Storyteller #3 - | The dog barked at the Billy Goat... |
| Dog - | Billy Goat, naughty Billy Goat...get out of our garden and stop eating our chiles! |
| Storyteller #2 - | And the Billy Goat just laughed and said... |
| Billy Goat - | Ha! Ha! Ha! No! No! No! |

| | |
|---|---|
| Storyteller #1 - | And with that, the Billy Goat flipped the dog into the air. |
| Storyteller #3 - | The farmer and his wife called their bull... |
| Farmer - | Bull, Bull! Help us get that Billy Goat out of our garden. |
| Farmer's Wife - | Make him stop eating our chiles! |
| Storyteller #2 - | So, the bull snorted at the Billy Goat... |
| Bull - | Billy Goat, naughty Billy Goat...get out of our garden and stop eating our chiles! |
| Storyteller #1 - | And the Billy Goat just laughed and said... |
| Billy Goat - | Ha! Ha! Ha! No! No! No! |

Storyteller #2 - And with that, the Billy goat flipped even the mighty bull into the air.

Storyteller #1 - Just then a little red ant spoke up. He had been watching the Billy Goat from a nearby leaf.

Little Red Ant - Maybe I can help get that naughty Billy Goat out of the garden.

Storyteller #3 - The Little Red Ant said to the farmer and his wife.

Farmer - You? You are so tiny.

Farmer's Wife - How can you help us?

Storyteller #1 - The farmer and his wife said to the ant.

Storyteller #2 - The Little Red Ant smiled and said...

Little Red Ant - Just watch and you will see.

Storyteller #3 - The Little Red Ant climbed onto the Billy Goat's tail. He crawled across the Billy Goat's back and onto his neck. Then the tiny fellow climbed right onto the Billy Goat's ear and bit the Billy Goat as hard as he could!

| | |
|---|---|
| Storyteller #2 - | The Billy Goat jumped into the air and said... |
| Billy Goat - | Ouch! Ouch! Ouch! Some big, gigantic, terrible thing just bit my ear! I'd better hurry and get away from here! |
| Storyteller #1 - | The Billy Goat ran out of the garden and was never seen again. |
| Storyteller #3 - | And the Little Red Ant smiled and said... |
| Little Red Ant - | Oh me, oh my! There is no one stronger than I! I may be small, but I am mighty...as mighty as can be! |
| All - | The End |
| Little Red Ant - | Adios! |

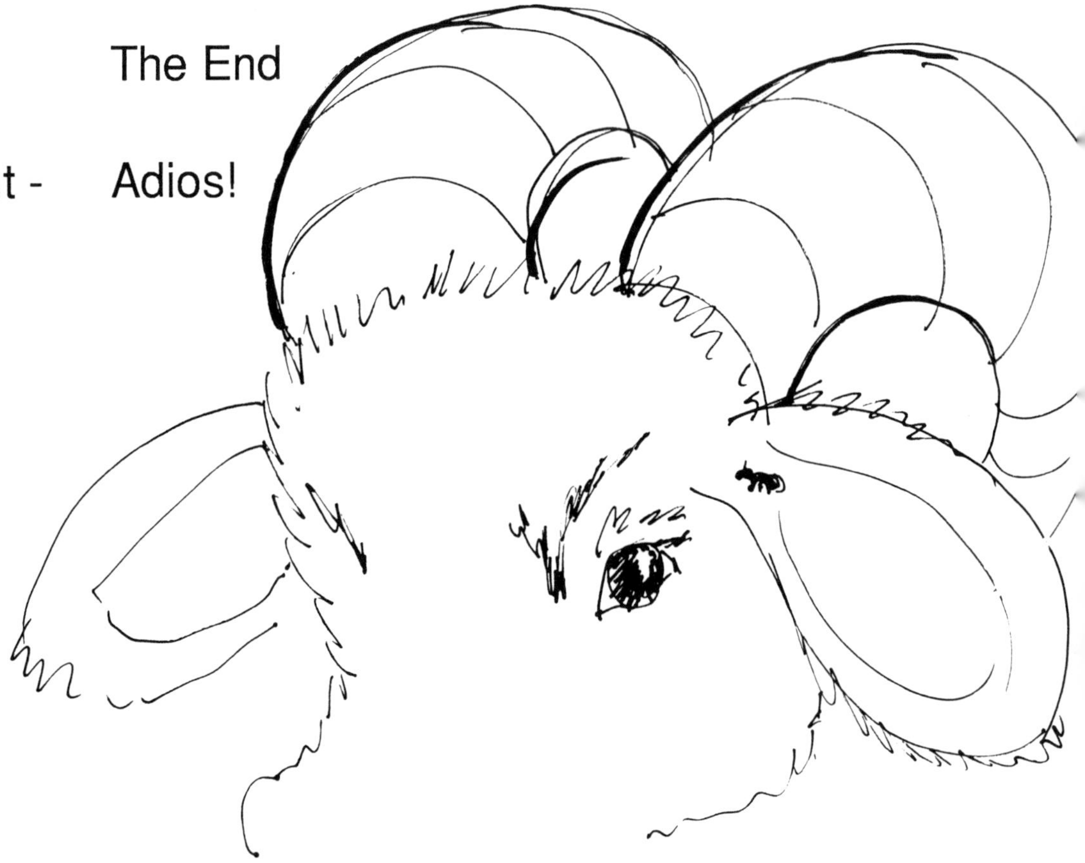

## Cooks in the Classroom!

- Here's a perfect way to share this script, some delicious food, and an appreciation for the Mexican culture all in one terrific lesson! Have students rehearse the script several times so that they are comfortable with their lines. Next, have students design invitations to a "mini" Mexican fiesta...(we invited our 6th grade buddies). Be sure to show students samples of Mexican art so that they can incorporate some of these patterns on their invitations. Students can prepare a sumptuous feast featuring Zucchini and Chiles Casserole, beans, and flan. A word about flan...we tried making it and had a soupy mess on our hands. (EEK!) Best bet?...use the packaged mixes available at most super markets. You'd think kids wouldn't like this being that it's all veggies...but they ate it all up and asked for more!

# Zucchini and Chiles Casserole Ole´

1 lb. extra lean ground beef
3 medium zucchinis, cut into thin slices
1/2 teaspoon salt
1 teaspoon chili powder
1 7 oz. can diced green chiles
1 package prepared Mexican rice (Rice-A-Roni Brand)
1 cup sour cream
2 cups shredded jack cheese
2 large tomatoes, chopped

- Saute´ the first 4 ingredients, then add the chiles, prepared rice mix, sour cream and 1 cup of the cheese. Place in a greased casserole. Top with chopped tomatoes and remaining cheese. Bake at 350º for 20-25 minutes. Mmmm...Ole´!

# *Favorite Mexican Folktales and Stories*

Hola! Super Readers! Be sure to hustle on down to your biblioteca (library) and read some of these terrific libros! (books) Have fun!

| | |
|---|---|
| • Borreguita and the Coyote | by Verna Aardema |
| • The Coyote Rings the Wrong Bell | by Francisco Mora |
| • The Boy Who Could Do Anything: And Other Mexican Folktales | by Anita Brenner |
| • The Riddle and the Drum | by Verna Aardema |
| • Uncle Nacho's Hat<br>El Sombrero del Tio Nacho | by Harriet Rohmer |
| • Cincuenta en la Cebra<br>Contando Con Los Animales -<br>Counting with the Animals | by Nancy Maria Grande Tabor |
| • The Fabulous Fireworks Family | by James Flora |
| • Listen to the Desert<br>Oye Al Desierto | by Pat Mora |

# The Lion's Share

## An African Folktale

A Reader's Theatre Script
Adapted by Lisa Blau

| | | |
|---|---|---|
| Reader #1 | Lion | Hyena Son #2 |
| Reader #2 | Father Hyena | |
| Reader #3 | Hyena Son #1 | |

Reader #1 - Long ago in the highlands of Africa there lived an old hyena and his sons.

Reader #2 - The father hyena stayed in his cave day and night to guard his home. Each night he sent his sons out to hunt for food.

Reader #3 - Now before he sent his sons out to hunt, the old hyena would say to them...

Father Hyena - My sons...you must be brave hunters. You must run fast and be strong-hearted fighters just like your father. You must make me proud.

| | |
|---|---|
| Hyena Son #1 - | Yes, yes father. We shall do as you ask. We will be strong and brave hunters. |
| Hyena Son #2 - | Yes, we will make you proud. We shall bring back a grand feast to prove ourselves strong and mighty. |
| Reader #1 - | The hyena sons told their father. |
| Reader #2 - | And so the hyena sons set out for the evening hunt. |
| Reader #3 - | By and by they met a lion. |
| Reader #1 - | Now the hyenas wanted nothing to do with this tawny-maned beast and began to walk away when the lion called out to them... |
| Lion - | Good evening, young friends! Why don't we search for food together tonight? I've been searching for hours, but I have been most unlucky. |
| Hyena #1 - | Well...we really like to hunt by ourselves. |
| Reader #2 - | The oldest hyena told the lion. |

| | |
|---|---|
| Lion - | But, my friends...we could catch more food between us and we could do it faster. Your keen sense of smell and my great strength will make the hunt an easy task. Whatever we catch, we will split evenly. |
| Reader #3 - | The clever lion said to the hyenas. Then the youngest hyena said... |
| Hyena #2 - | We should join the lion in tonight's hunt. His plan sounds like a good one. |
| Reader #1 - | So, the lion and the young hyenas set out to catch their evening meal. |
| Reader #2 - | Luck was with the trio for soon the hyena's sharp noses led them to a flock of guinea hens. |

| | |
|---|---|
| Reader #2 - | And with the lion's great strength, they soon caught all of the hens. |
| Lion - | Now my young friends, you see how wise it was for us to hunt together this evening. |
| Reader #2 - | The lion told the hyenas. Then the lion smiled and said... |

| | |
|---|---|
| Lion - | And now we shall share our catch. |
| Reader #1 - | The lion took all of the hens except for the smallest hen which he tossed to the hyenas. |
| Lion - | What's the matter my friends? Didn't I share these evenly? |
| Reader #2 - | The lion said to the young hyenas. |
| Reader #3 - | When the old hyena saw his sons' catch, he growled and said... |
| Old Hyena - | Do you call this pile of feathers a meal? |
| Reader #2 - | The old hyena scolded his sons for over an hour. He ended his speech with... |
| Old Hyena - | I am a mighty and strong hunter. You both must work harder. I am <u>very</u> ashamed of you. |
| Hyena #1 - | But father, we had a good catch. You see, tonight we hunted with the lion. He said we would share our hunt. But the lion took all of the hens for himself and left us with just one. |

Reader #1 - The young hyena told his angry father.

Reader #2 - The news made the old hyena even more angry. He yelled loudly at his sons...

Old Hyena - You cowards! You fools! Follow me. I shall show you how to deal with that lion. He will not make me look like a fool. Afterall, I am a mighty and strong hunter.

Reader #2 - So, the old hyena picked up the hen and walked to the lion's den.

Reader #3 - When he saw the lion, the old hyena called out...

Old Hyena - Lion! Lion! Come out, come out! I must speak to you at once!

Reader #1 - The lion had been sleeping and he did not like to be awakened from his nap. The lion stood up and walked to the edge of his den.

Lion - ROAR! Who dares to wake me?!

Reader #2 - The lion glared at the old hyena. His mane stood up on edge. He looked very strong, very mighty...but most of all...very angry.

Reader #3 - Then the lion said...

Lion - Well, old hyena...do you want something?

Old Hyena - I...I...I...you see...I...er...

Reader #1 - The old hyena was so frightened by the lion that he did not know what to say. At last he said...

Old Hyena - My sons told me how you shared your food with them. You are much too kind and generous. We came here to give you this hen. This is for you.

Reader #1 - So, the hyena gave the last hen to the lion.

Reader #2 - And with that, the old hyena walked away.

Reader #3 - And never again did the old hyena boast about his strength and bravery.

All - The End

## ♥ TRIED - AND - TRUE TERRIFIC TEACHING STRATEGIES ♥

- Prior to reading the script, discuss the history of African folktales with your students. Each tribal group in Africa passed down stories from generation to generation. Many African folktales, like the fables of Aesop and the folktales of the Native Americans, have a moral or lesson to be learned.

- To further enhance your unit on African folktales, visit your public library and ask for the <u>outstanding</u> video, "A Story, A Story". This video, based on the retelling of the African folktale by Gail E. Haley features authentic African music and brilliantly colored African wood cuts. A treat for your students eyes and ears! To order this and other folktales on video contact: Weston Woods 1-800-243-5020. Don't miss <u>Why Mosquitoes Buzz in People's Ears</u> by Verna Aardema also available on video by Weston Woods!

- Art! Art! Art! Your students will enjoy designing their own African wood cuts. All you'll need are some flat pieces of styrofoam from meat trays. Cut the meat trays into rectangles that measure about 3 inches by 3 inches. Share some samples of African wood cut patterns and then instruct students to "sketch" their own patterns onto the styrofoam pieces using an opened paper clip. To make prints, use a brayer and tempera paints. For a special effect, have students stamp the African wood cuts as a border on brown craft paper. Students can then make colorful cut outs of their favorite part of this script using construction paper scraps. These are magnificent!

- Write! Write! Write! Have students write facts and information about lions or hyenas using the African wood cut paper. Or you may wish to have students create a new ending for the story. What would have happened if the father hyena stood up to the lion? The students can use their African wood print paper for this creative writing assignment.

- Music! Music! Music! Award winning children's performer Ella Jenkins has many excellent recordings featuring African music. Look for, "Jambo and Other Call and Response Songs and Chants" and "Adventures in Rhythm". These can be found at most any teacher supply store or they can be ordered from Learning is Fun 1-800-290-5437.

- Read! Read! Read! A booklist featuring a variety of African titles is included in this unit. Send this list home with students. Encourage families to share these wonderful books together. Don't forget to send home the script, "The Lion's Share" for students to read and perform for their families. What fun!

- Some final thoughts...If you and your class are planning to perform "The Lion's Share" for other classes, here are a few ideas to enhance your performance:

  1. Send invitations using the African woodcut paper.

  2. Play authentic African music as your guests enter.

  3. Paint a brightly colored mural for readers to stand in front of as they perform the script.

  4. Pass out copies of the "African Stories Too Good to Miss" booklist.

  5. Serve tasty African Banana Fritters.

# African Banana Fritters

3 very ripe bananas, peeled and mashed
3/4 c. milk
2 eggs
1/2 c. granulated sugar
1 c. flour

**Directions:** Combine the flour and sugar, then add eggs and milk. Stir in the mashed banana. Using your hands, form fritters using about 2 tablespoons of the mixture for each fritter. Fry in hot oil for 2-3 minutes...just until the fritters turn a golden brown. Drain on paper towels. Sprinkle with powdered sugar and serve warm. What a tasty treat!

# African Stories Too Good To Miss

Dear Super Readers,

I know that you will REALLY enjoy these <u>wonderful</u> stories from Africa. Some are folktales and some tell about the people who live in Africa. Be sure to ask the librarian to help you find these and other books. Happy Reading!

| | |
|---|---|
| Anansi the Spider | by Gerald McDermott |
| Anansi and the Moss-Covered Rock | by Eric Kimmel |
| Bringing the Rain to Kapiti Plain | by Verna Aardema |
| Oh, Koji! How Could You? | by Verna Aardema |
| Moja Means One | by Tom and Muriel Feelings |
| Jambo Means Hello | by Tom and Muriel Feelings |
| Wood-Hoopoe Willie | by Virginia Kroll |
| I am Eyes Ni Macho | by Leila Ward |
| Bury My Bones But Keep My Words - African Tales for Retelling | by Tom Fairman |
| Jafta | by Hugh Lewin |
| Jafta's Mother | by Hugh Lewin |
| Jafta's Father | by Hugh Lewin |

CUT OUT
CUT OUT

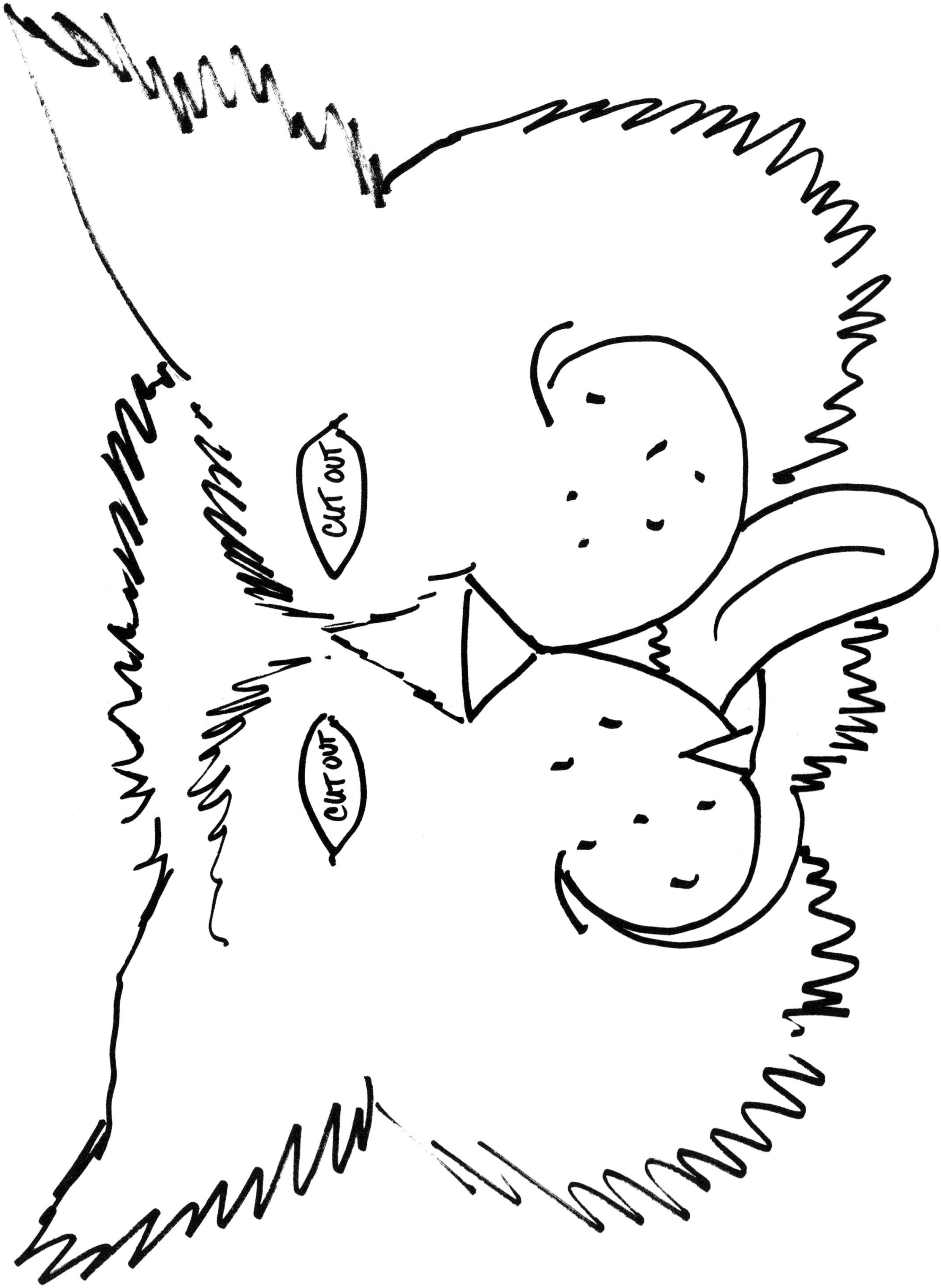
CUT OUT
CUT OUT

# *The Rabbit and the Turtle*

*A Cherokee Folktale*

A Reader's Theatre Script
Adapted by Lisa Blau

| Storyteller #1 | Storyteller #2 | Storyteller #3 |
|---|---|---|
| Rabbit | Turtle | |

Storyteller #1 - Good morning. Welcome to our presentation.

Storyteller #2 - Today you are in for a real treat. You will hear a folktale from the Cherokee people. This story was told many, many years ago.

Storyteller #3 - The Cherokee were a woodland tribe. They hunted in the forests and fished in the streams of the Appalachian Mountains.

Storyteller #2 - The Cherokees were expert farmers. They planted corn, squash, pumpkins, and beans. The women tended to the crops.

Storyteller #1 - The Cherokees built homes from logs, tree bark, and grass. The chief's house was usually in the center of the village.

Storyteller #3 - The Cherokee people were hardworking and peaceful. They rarely fought with other tribes.

Storyteller #2 - The Cherokee people cared deeply about one another and about nature. Their stories often have important messages. Today you will hear about a boastful rabbit who is outsmarted by a very wise turtle.

Storyteller #1 - And the name of our story is...

All - The Rabbit and the Turtle.

Storyteller #3 - Long, long ago everyone knew that the rabbit was a great runner. Rabbit would boast and brag to the other animals about his great speed.

Storyteller #2 - Everyone also knew about the turtle. The turtle was a very slow animal, the slowest in the forest.

Storyteller #1 - One day when rabbit began to once again boast about his great speed, the turtle, who was tired of all of rabbit's talk said...

Turtle - Let us have a race. We can race across four mountains. The first one to cross over the final ridge will be the winner.

Storyteller #3 - The rabbit could not believe his ears. A race with turtle would be so easy to win. So rabbit replied...

Rabbit - Oh, turtle, you know you cannot run. You may have a head start over the first mountain ridge.

Storyteller #2 - Turtle agreed to rabbit's plan and said...

Turtle - Let us meet here tomorrow morning and then our race can begin.

Storyteller #1 - Rabbit dashed home. But turtle had other plans. He sent for his friends and family.

Turtle - Rabbit and I will have a race tomorrow. I know that I cannot outrun the rabbit, but I have a plan that should teach that boastful rabbit a lesson.

Storyteller #3 - Turtle told his family and friends.

Storyteller #2 - All of turtle's friends agreed to help with the plan. All of the animals came to watch the race. As planned, turtle was given a head start over the first ridge.

Storyteller #3 - Rabbit dashed over the first ridge and said...

Rabbit - I'll pass that slow old turtle in no time at all.

Storyteller #1 - But much to rabbit's surprise, he saw turtle going over the next ridge.

Storyteller #2 - Rabbit raced over the second ridge and said...

Rabbit - Ah! I'll pass up that old turtle this time!

Storyteller #3 - But once again, rabbit saw turtle going over the next ridge.

Storyteller #1 - So, rabbit raced over the third ridge and said...

Rabbit - I'll pass the turtle on this ridge for sure!

Storyteller #2 - But as rabbit came down the other side of the ridge, he saw turtle cross over the fourth ridge and win the race!

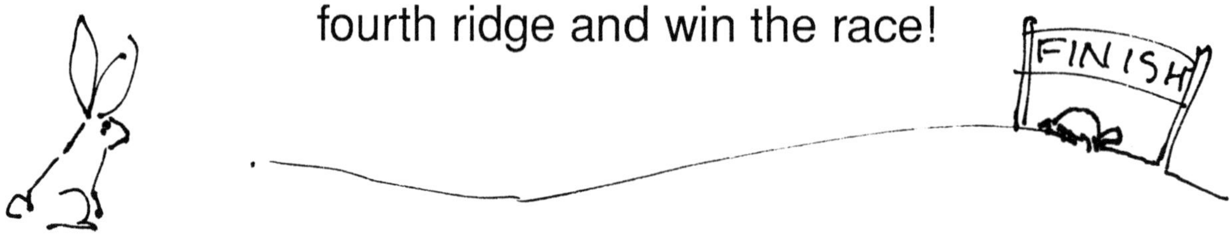

| | |
|---|---|
| Storyteller #2 - | Rabbit could not believe his eyes! How could the turtle, who moves so slowly have won the race? |
| Turtle - | It was an easy race. I asked my family and friends to help me climb each ridge. You see, we all look alike, so each one of us climbed a different ridge. |
| All - | And that is how the turtle taught rabbit that it is not a good thing to boast and brag. |
| Rabbit - | The End |

## ♥ TRIED - AND - TRUE TERRIFIC TEACHING STRATEGIES ♥

- As a pre-reading activity, you may wish to share a few Native American folktales with your students. A complete listing of titles can be found in this unit. You can also explain that as with so many other cultures, Native American stories were handed down from generation to generation. Your students will enjoy comparing this Native American story to Aesop's fable, The Tortoise and the Hare. For more comparisons, be sure to share, Doctor Coyote: Native American Aesop Fables by John Bierhorst.

- Provide your students with information about the Cherokee people. Our students tend to think that all Native Americans lived in teepees and hunted buffalo. Two outstanding books about the Cherokee people are: The Cherokee by Barbara A. McCall - Rourke Publications (ISBN #0-86625-376-9) and The Cherokee by Emilie U. Lepthien - Children's Press (ISBN #0516-0119388-4).

- Joseph Bruchac is one of today's finest Native American storytellers and writers. As you and your students share Native American folktales, you'll want to use Bruchac's excellent book, Native American Animal Stories. This is a wonderful collection of stories, maps, and illustrations. This book can be ordered from:

  Fulcrum Publishing<br>
  350 Indiana Street<br>
  Golden, CO 80401

- Bruchac's latest book, The First Strawberries (ISBN # 0-8037-1331-2) is a Cherokee tale full of wisdom and beauty. It's messages about respect between men and women and the gifts given to us by the earth are indeed powerful. This is a book that merits lots of discussion time as children take in the book's many messages. Strawberry patterns are included here for students to write about someone special in their lives. Mount the completed berries on red and pink construction paper and hang all around your classroom's door frames. Now as students enter and exit your classroom they'll have an opportunity to read and admire some "berry" special creations.

# Cooks in the Classroom!

Corn was a very important part of the Cherokee's diet. The Cherokee women used corn husks to weave floor mats and, as noted in the script, the Cherokee women also planted and harvested the corn. Knowing how much children enjoy cooking, a recipe for corn meal muffins is included in this unit.

## Corn Meal Muffins

Note: This recipe will make 2 small muffins. To make this cooking experience quick, easy, and fun, simply place all ingredients in an "assembly line" set-up and post the recipe on the board for students to read and follow.

Sift Together:
1 cup flour
3 T. sugar
1 1/2 t. baking powder
1/2 t. salt

Then Add:
2 T. milk
1 egg, beaten
2 t. oil

Next: Stir the ingredients together just to moisten then pour into muffin tins that have been lined with greased corn husks. (Rub oil on corn husks...these are available in most grocery stores in the Mexican foods section.)

Bake: 10 minutes at 400°.

# Native American Folktales

- Ikotomi and the Berries — by Paul Goble
- The Girl Who Loved Wild Horses — by Paul Goble
- Star Boy — by Paul Goble
- How the Loon Lost Her Voice — by Anne Cameron
- Raven — by Gerald McDermott

- The Story of Jumping Mouse — by John Steptoe
- Tonwey and the Eagles and Other Lakota Tales — by Rosebud Yellow Robe
- Ma'ii and Cousin Horned Toad A Traditional Navajo Story — by Shonto Begay
- The Chase A Kutenai Indian Tale — by Beatrice Tanaka
- Native American Animal Stories — by Joseph Bruchac
- The Prince and the Salmon People — by Claire Rudolf Murphy
- Coyote Stories for Children — by Susan Strauss

♥ Write a special loving note to someone who is "berry" special to you.

# Jack and the Beanstalk

## An English Folktale

A Reader's Theatre Script
Adapted by Lisa Blau

| | | |
|---|---|---|
| Jack | Reader #1 | Little Man |
| Mother | Reader #2 | Giant's Wife |
| Giant | Reader #3 | |

Reader #1 - Once upon a time long, long ago there lived a young boy named Jack.

Reader #2 - Jack lived in a small cottage with his mother. They were <u>very</u> poor.

Reader #3 - One day Jack's mother said to him...

Mother - Oh, Jack. Whatever will we do? We haven't any money for food. You will have to go to town and sell our cow. It is the only way that we'll be able to eat.

Jack - Very well, mother.

| | |
|---|---|
| Reader #1 - | So, Jack took the cow and walked towards the town. |
| Reader #2 - | He hadn't gone far when he met a strange little man. |
| Little Man - | Say...young lad...where are you going with that cow? |
| Jack - | I'm going to town to sell the cow so we can buy some food. |
| Little Man - | Ah...but the town is so very far away...I will gladly buy the cow from you. |
| Jack - | What price will you pay me for my cow? |
| Little Man - | I have no coins...but...I have something far better than money. If you give me your cow...I shall give you some magic beans! |

| | |
|---|---|
| Jack - | Well, I don't know if I should. My mother told me to go to town and sell the cow. |
| Little Man - | But, lad! Think how proud your mother will be when she learns that you have some magic beans! |
| Jack - | Very well then. Here is the cow. Please let me have your magic beans. |

Reader #3 - So, the deal was made. Jack walked home with his sack of magic beans. His mother would be so proud of him for making such a good deal.

Mother - Well, Jack. Did you get a good price for our cow?

Jack - Yes, I did. I got this sack of magic beans!

Mother - What? You foolish, foolish boy! How could you have done such a thing? Now we have no food to eat, whatever will we do?

Reader #1 - So, Jack's mother sent Jack to bed without any supper and she threw the bag of magic seeds out the window.

Reader #2 - In the morning when Jack awoke there was a huge beanstalk growing outside his window.

Jack - Wow! Look at this beanstalk! Why it seems to touch the clouds!

Reader #1 - So, Jack decided to climb up the beanstalk.

Reader #2 - He climbed and climbed and climbed.

Reader #1 - At last he reached the top. He was in a magical land.

Reader #2 - So, Jack found a large, beautiful castle. He knocked on the door. A woman opened the huge door.

Giant's Wife - Who are you? What do you want, boy?

Jack - I'm Jack. I've just climbed up the beanstalk. I'm very hungry. Could you spare some food for me, kind woman?

Giant's Wife - Very well, come in...but, be careful! My husband is a mean and grumpy giant. He will not be happy to see you.

Reader #3 - So, Jack went into the kitchen and the Giant's wife fed him a good meal.

Reader #2 - All at once the floor began to shake and a loud voice roared...

Giant - FE-FI-FO-FUM! I smell the blood of an Englishman! Be he alive or be he dead, I'll grind his bones to make my bread!

Giant's Wife - Oh, heavens! The giant has returned! Quick, hide here in the cupboard.

Reader #2 - Jack hid in the cupboard and watched

what the giant did next.

Giant - Wife! Wife! Bring me some food, my gold, my magic hen, and golden harp! Hurry, hurry! Do as I say.

Reader #1 - The giant ate and ate and ate. He counted his many bags of gold.

Reader #2 - Then the giant roared at the magic hen...

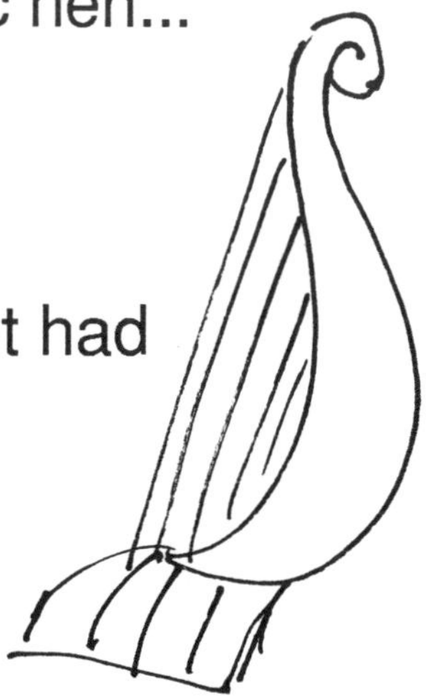

Giant - Lay me ten golden eggs at once!

Reader #1 - And the magic hen did as the giant had ordered.

Giant - Play magic harp, play!

Reader #2 - The Magic Harp began to play the sweetest music that Jack had ever heard.

Reader #1 - Soon the giant fell asleep. His loud snores shook the castle.

Reader #2 - Jack saw his chance to run away.

Reader #1 - But before he left, Jack grabbed the giant's sack of gold, his hen and the magic harp.

Reader #2 - But as Jack picked up the magic hen, the hen cried out and woke the giant up.

Reader #1 - Jack ran as fast as he could out of the castle and across the clouds to the beanstalk.

Reader #2 - The giant ran after Jack. His great steps shook the ground.

Reader #1 - Jack scurried down the beanstalk. The giant was not far behind him.

Reader #2 - When Jack reached the ground he grabbed an axe and began to chop down the beanstalk.

Reader #3 - Hack! Hack! Hack! The ax flew across the beanstalk. At last the beanstalk fell to the ground and the mean and grumpy giant crashed down with it.

Reader #1 - That was the end of the magic beanstalk and the mean and grumpy giant. But it does not mean the end of our tale.

Reader #2 - Oh no! Our tale has the happiest of endings, for Jack and his mother now had all the money they needed.

Reader #3 - They also had a hen that laid golden eggs...

Reader #1 - And a harp to play the world's sweetest music...

Reader #2 - And they lived happily ever after.

All - The End

- Read! Read! Read! Ask students to be detectives and search for as many different retellings of Jack and the Beanstalk as they can find. Read and share the many different versions and discuss with your students all of the similarities and differences between the retellings. These comparisons can be placed onto a chart. One of our favorite retellings is:

  - Jack and the Beanstalk
    Retold in Verse for Boys and Girls to Read Themselves
    by Beatrice Schenk de Regniers
    (Aladdin Books • ISBN # 0-689-71421-1)

- Science! Science! Science! Have a bean race! This is a terrific activity that will combine science and math and will most certainly spark your students' interests. Soak several kinds of beans overnight. (You might try using scarlet runner beans, lentils, yellow wax beans and red beans.)

- Plant beans in pots about one inch deep and water until the soil is moist. Watch out! Kids tend to drown seeds which will cause them to rot...YUCK!...the voice of experience is speaking here! Place beans in a sunny spot or in a wagon that can be moved outside each day. It should take about four days for your beans to sprout.

- Have students record the growth of their bean plants on a graph. We named each of our plants for easier identification. This proved to be great fun whenever visitors came to our classroom because the children would all say, "Come meet Curly, Fluffy, Greeny and Jack." (Where did we ever come up with that last name?!)

- For further investigations into plant growth, have students observe and sketch the growth of the bean plants as the weeks progress. At the end of the third week, discuss the results of the graph and have students share their drawings and observations. Which plant grew fastest? How tall is the tallest plant? How tall is the smallest plant? How many days did it take for the first bean to sprout? Write a group story based upon the results recorded on your graph. Staple each students' individual graph, sketches and observation notes into a green construction paper folder. Students can take these folders home to share with their families.

- Cooks in the Classroom! A tasty recipe for bean salad and sweet and sour dressing are included in this unit. I love to send recipes home for my students to prepare as a homework assignment. Cooking is a life skill that our students need. With more and more latch-key children in our classrooms, we need to give homework that is meaningful and purposeful. In addition, cooking activities provide children with the opportunity to use many skills such as reading, counting, and measuring. Best of all...it's homework that I don't have to correct!

# Three Bean Super Keen Salad

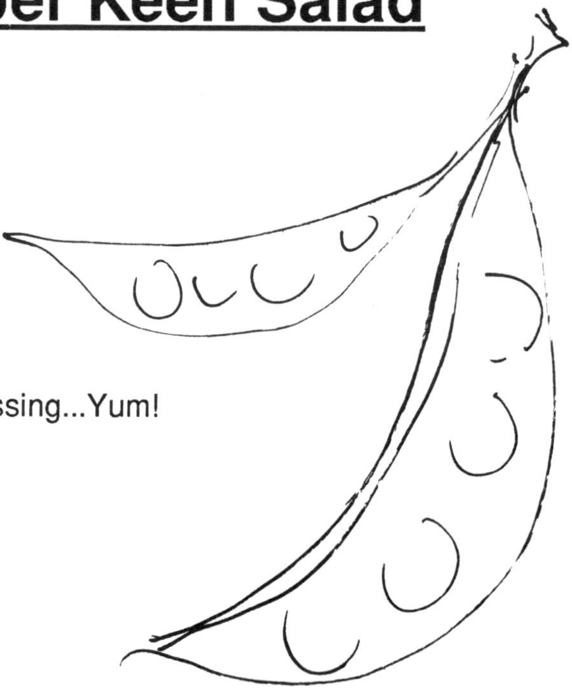

Count:
10 canned kidney beans
10 canned garbanzo beans
10 canned green beans
5 pieces of chopped celery
1 TBSP chopped green onion
1 TBSP chopped fresh parsley
1 TBSP chopped green pepper

Mix together with Tangy Sweet and Sour Dressing...Yum!

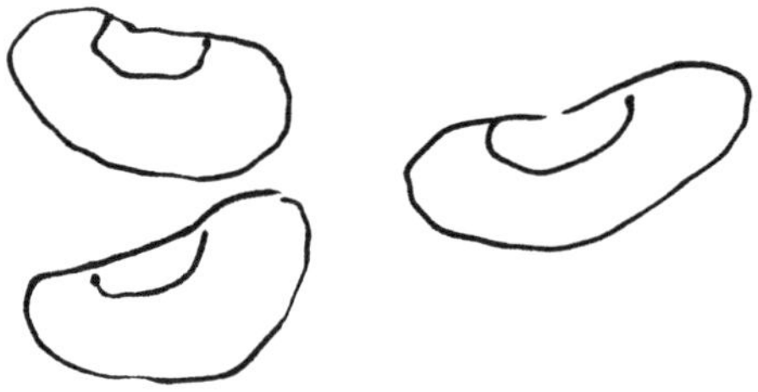

# Tangy Sweet and Sour Dressing

Mix these ingredients together in a bowl:

1 TBSP granulated sugar
1/2 tsp. salt
1 TBSP vinegar
2 TBSP salad oil
1 tsp. lemon juice
1 tsp. pepper

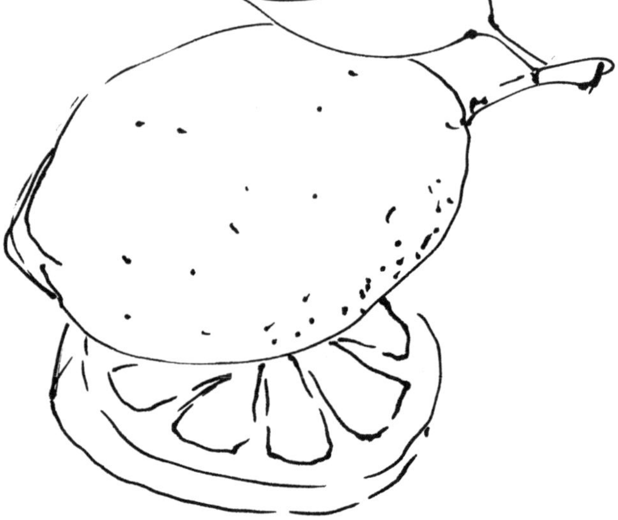

# *Resources! Resources! Resources!*

- Now that you are TOTALLY hooked on sharing folktales with your students, you may wish to check out these fabulous resources:

- Skipping Stones
  A Multicultural Children's quarterly
  P.O. Box 3939
  Eugene, Oregon  97403-0939
  (503) 342-4956
  Skipping Stones is a non-profit, children's magazine that features stories from around the world. Many of the stories are written by children...your students can submit their stories and artwork! Many stories emphasize racial harmony and taking care of the earth. A single issue costs $5.00 and a full subscription (4 issues) is only $20.00. A welcome addition to any classroom or school library.

- NAPPS (National Association for the Preservation and Perpetuation of Storytelling)
  Box 309
  Jonesborough, TN 37659
  1-615-753-2171
  You'll discover the joys of storytelling for you and your students. Membership includes a subscription to the NAPPS marvelous newsletter, Yarnspinner.

- Handbook for Storytellers
  by Caroline Feller Bauer
  Countless ideas for bringing folktales alive in our classrooms.
  You can order this book from:
  Mulberry, A Bookshop for Children
  169 Fountain Avenue
  Pacific Grove, CA  93950
  1-408-375-3016

- American Library Association
  50 E. Huron Street
  Chicago, IL 60611
  Ask for one of their catalogs - lots of GREAT books and their wonderful READ posters featuring all kinds of celebrities.

- Children's Book Council
  568 Broadway #404
  New York, New York 10012
  Ask for their catalog - many outstanding resource books and reading incentive ideas.

- International Reading Association
  1-800-336-READ
  Join this professional organization and you'll receive their <u>fabulous</u> publication entitled "Reading Today".

- National Council of Teachers of English
  111 Kenyon Road
  Urbana, IL 61820
  Join this professional organization and you'll receive their publication plus information on conferences in your area. Learn who NCTE will name this year's top children's poet! (The winner is announced each February)

- <u>Children Around the World</u>
  The Instant Bulletin Board Book
  Teacher's Friend Publications • 1-800-843-9680
  What a neat resourcebook! The book includes a Ready-To-Use interactive mural and a complete Teacher's Guide!

This Super Reader's Award
is presented to
for outstanding reading.
CONGRATULATIONS!
teacher's signature
SUPER
READER

# I've Read Around the World!!!

BRAVO!
Bravo!
BRAVO!
Bravo!
BRAVO!
Bravo!
BRAVO!
Bravo!
BRAVO!
Bravo!
BRAVO!

This certificate is presented to

____________________________________

for having read all of the folktale scripts from around the world.

Congratulations!

Signed, __________________________

Date __________________

♥♥ *One from the Heart* ♥♥

## STAFF DEVELOPMENT WORKSHOPS by *LISA BLAU*, M.A.

AUTHOR & EDUCATIONAL CONSULTANT

IF YOU'RE LOOKING FOR A DYNAMIC, ENTHUSIASTIC, AND MOTIVATING STAFF DEVELOPMENT CONSULTANT *or* CONFERENCE KEYNOTE SPEAKER CALL **800-292-6202** FOR MORE INFORMATION ABOUT *LISA* COMING TO ***your*** SCHOOL!!

### FOR EDUCATORS....

- Learn how to enhance your language arts program through effective research-based strategies and methods.
- Discover how to create a dynamic writing program emphasizing writing as a process.
- Learn how to design a **balanced** curriculum which draws its strength from the best of both phonics-based and literature-based instruction.
- Learn the best strategies to use with Title I students - ideas that can be implemented immediately in any classroom.
- Discover easy ways to incorporate literature into your math program with strategies based upon the NCTM standards.
- Mrs. Blau's presentations emphasize issues such as scheduling, spelling, assessment, and multicultural programs.
- Learn how to use literature, hands-on experiments, and at-home family activities to enhance your science program.
- A Staff Development program specifically designed to meet the needs and interests of your school's teachers can easily be arranged.
- Mrs. Blau's **parent presentations** are an ideal way to help parents gain new ideas to help their children with at-home learning--particularly Title I families.

### About *Lisa Blau*, M.A....

**Educator-consultant Lisa Blau has an extensive background in the field of education. Mrs. Blau has been a classroom teacher, a Title I Resource Specialist, a member of the gifted program teaching team, and a Mentor Teacher. Her wealth of knowledge regarding the most effective strategies for teaching reading and writing led to a five-year position as a mentor. In this capacity, Mrs. Blau trained K-6 teachers on the use of balanced reading instruction and the most effective methods for teaching basic skills, including phonics and spelling. She also appeared on the Educational Television Network's programs featuring the use of literature across the curriculum.**

**Mrs. Blau currently provides staff development training for teachers across the United States, as well as serving as an adjunct professor at Seattle Pacific University. While combining educational research and theory, her presentations provide educators with highly practical strategies and ideas that focus on some of today's pressing issues, such as spelling and phonics. She offers educators basic teaching skills, including the best ways to motivate children to become lifelong readers and writers. Mrs. Blau shares the most effective and current methods for reading and writing instruction, while offering teachers a vast array of creative teaching tools.**

**A frequent featured speaker at conferences across the United States, Mrs. Blau has received high marks from her audiences at the following conferences:**

- **International Reading Association**
- **National Science Teachers Association**
- **California Reading Association**
- **Southwest Regional self-esteem Association**
- **Oregon Reading Association**
- **Washington Reading Association**

**Mrs. Blau is the recipient of the prestigious "Celebrate Literacy Award" from the International Reading Association for her many contributions to the promotion of literacy and learning.**

**She is the author of several Readers' Theatre resource books featuring scripts and extended activities designed to help students discover the joy of reading. An avid reader, Mrs. Blau is happiest when she can read to her two children, Daniel and Kayla.**

# More Outstanding Resources...

*Literature Based Math Ideas!*

**It All Adds Up.......................................$9.95**
If you are looking for a way to enhance your math program, then this is THE book for you!!! You'll find literature-based math strategies based upon some of today's best-loved children's books. There are reproducible activity pages, scores of graphing and estimation activities, plus plenty of classroom-tested recipes that your students will LOVE!!!

**ORDER TOLL FREE** | **CALL 1-800-292-6202** | **VISA & MASTERCARD**

*Reproducible Activity Pages*

**Learning with Literature.......................$9.95**
You'll find a plethora of creative teaching ideas to use with some of today's best loved children's books. There are easy-to-follow Into, Through, and Beyond strategies to use with each piece of literature that is highlighted in this book. There are also reproducible pages to use for creating class books or individual Literature Logs with your students. I have selected books that will enhance virtually every part of the curriculum including math, science, social studies, and multicultural education.

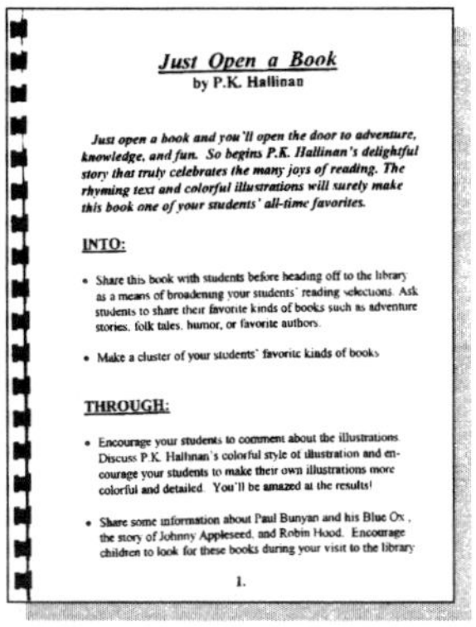


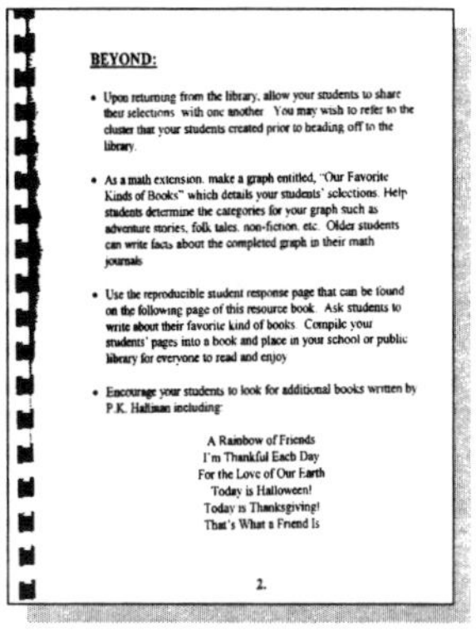

**Fall is Fabulous...................................................$10.95**
Start your school year off with "oodles" of fun when you share the many scripts and activities featuring all of your favorite fall themes including Johnny Appleseed, batty bats, hooty owls and spindly spiders! Your students will **love** the fabulously funny Halloween play plus all the other scripts.

**Winter is Wonderful..........................................$10.95**
You can chase away winter's chill with Winter is Wonderful. Scripts include Happy Ground Hog's Day, They Called Him Honest Abe, The Story of Benjamin Franklin, plus many more! Your students will FLIP over the super "sweet" play for Valentine's Day!

**Ideal to use with Primary Grades, Title I, and Special Education Students**

**Welcome Spring...................................................$9.95**
Ah...my favorite season of the year celebrated with wonderful scripts including Ducks, Ducks, Ducks!, Busy Body Bugs, and Bouncing Bunnies. There's also a DARLING play for Mother's Day plus many more exciting ideas in this marvelous resource book.

**History is a Story Well Told................................$9.95**
Reader's Theatre scripts and activities created to enhance your social studies program!!! Your students will delight in learning about Martin Luther King, Jr., Helen Keller, and the Statue of Liberty. Enjoy these scripts plus many more!

**Favorite Folktales & Fabulous Fables..............$10.95**
This book is a must for teachers looking for ways to enhance their multicultural programs. Scripts include Jack and the Beanstalk, The One Inch Boy (Japan), and The Billy Goat and the Chiles (Mexico). You will travel the globe with the exciting scripts and activities in this super book.

**Super Science...................................................$10.95**
Soar into the universe, peek under rocks, make "dinolicious" cookies, a real volcano and explore the other wonders of our world in Super Science, the resource book guaranteed to make your students have a "blast" reading.

**Countless Literature-Based Strategies ♥ Ready-To-Use-Tomorrow Activities ♥ Perforated Pages-Easy to Reproduce**

**Animals, Animals, Animals!...............................$9.95**
This book is an animal lover's delight! Scripts include: Bears, Eagles, Snails, and Big Cats. You'll be able to enhance your literature-based science program with flair when you share the scripts and extended activities in this book with your students.

**Good Enough to Eat!!!........................................$9.95**
Here's a tasty collection of scripts and extended activities that your students will really LOVE!!! Scripts include: The Magic Porridge Pot, Stone Soup, Popcorn! Popcorn! Popcorn! and many more. There is also a script about good nutrition. You'll use this valuable resource often!

# *ONE FROM THE HEART ♥ ORDER FORM*

**14150 N.E. 20th Street, Suite 223, Bellevue, Wa. 98007**
**1-800-292-6202/Fax 425-861-6319**

## RESOURCE BOOKS BY CONSULTANT LISA BLAU

isa Blau has written several exciting resource books featuring the use of Reader's Theatre. Each book contains a variety of scripts and xtended activities. There are recipes, writing ideas, production tips, and countless strategies that span the curriculum. If you are looking for an nnovative way to truly motivate your students, then be sure to try any of the ideas presented in these fabulous books!!!

---

Is your school or district in need of fresh and innovative ideas for a dynamite K-5 Staff Development workshop ? Lisa Blau, educational consultant, author and recipient of the prestigious "Celebrate Literacy" Award sponsored by the International Reading Council, will share with you exciting strategies to motivate your students to read and write!! Call 800-292-6202 for more information and dates available! One to five-day summer workshops also are available.

♥If you are responsible for booking Lisa Blau into your school, you will RECEIVE $50 in BOOKS !!

---

all is Fabulous! (Reader's Theatre Scripts)
tart your school year off with **oodles** of fun when you share the many scripts in this newly revised and updated resource book. You'll find scripts nd extended activities featuring all of your favorite fall themes including **Johnny Appleseed**, **bats**, **owls**, and **spiders**. Your students will **LOVE** the abulously funny Halloween play plus all of the many other scripts, recipes, and poems featured in this terrific resource book. ($10.95)

Vinter Is Wonderful! (Reader's Theatre Scripts)
You can chase away winter's chill with this newly revised and updated resource book. Scripts include: **Happy Groundhog's Day**, **They Called Him Honest Abe**, **The Story of Benjamin Franklin**, plus many more!!! Your students will **FLIP** over the super-sweet play for **Valentine's Day!** ($10.95)

Velcome Spring! (Reader's Theatre Scripts)
h...my favorite season of the year celebrated with wonderful scripts including **Ducks, Ducks, Ducks!**, **Busy Body Bugs**, and **Bouncing Bunnies**. here's also a **DARLING** play for **Mother's Day** plus many more exciting ideas in this marvelous resource book. ($9.95)

Animals! Animals! Animals! (Reader's Theatre Scripts)
his book is an animals lover's delight! Scripts include: **Bears**, **Eagles**, **Snails**, and **Big Cats**. You'll be able to enhance your literature-based cience program with flair when you share the scripts and extended activities in this book with your students. ($9.95)

ood Enough to Eat! (Reader's Theatre Scripts)
Here's a tasty collection of scripts and extended activities that your students will really **LOVE!!!** Scripts include: **The Magic Porridge Pot**, **Stone Soup**, **Popcorn! Popcorn! Popcorn!** and many more! There is also a script about good nutrition. You'll use this valuable resource often! ($9.95)

avorite Folktales and Fabulous Fables (Reader's Theatre Scripts)
Recently revised and expanded, this book is a must for teachers looking for ways to enhance their multicultural programs. Scripts include: **Jack and the Beanstalk**, **The One Inch Boy (Japan)**, and **The Billy Goats and the Chiles (Mexico)**. You will span the globe in this super book. ($10.95)

Super Science! (Reader's Theatre Scripts)
**Reader's Theatre** scripts with extended activities including at-home science experiment pages, recipes, and reproducible blackline master activity pages. Scripts include: **Volcanoes**, **The Solar System**, **Dazzling Dinosaurs**, **Geology**, and many more! ($10.95)

History is a Story Well Told (Reader's Theatre Scripts)
**Reader's Theatre** scripts and activities created to enhance your social studies program!!! Your students will delight in learning about **Martin Luther King, Jr.**, **Helen Keller**, and the **Statue of Liberty**. Enjoy these scripts plus many more! ($9.95)

t All Adds Up!
his unique resource book offers teachers countless strategies for implementing a literature-based math program. Graphing ideas plus plenty of eproducible pages are included in this book. Don't miss it!!! ($9.95)

earning with Literature
isa's latest book features detailed lesson plans and plenty of reproducible activity pages based on some of today's best loved children's books. ncludes such favorites as: **Life is Fun**, **Children Just Like Me**, **My Friends**, and **The Flag We Love**. ORDER today! ($9.95)

| Qty | ♥REQUESTS♥ | Price | TOTAL | Qty | ♥ *LISA BLAU'S BOOKS* ♥ | Price | TOTAL |
|---|---|---|---|---|---|---|---|
| | | | | | Fall Is Fabulous | 10.95 | |
| | | | | | Winter Is Wonderful | 10.95 | |
| | | | | | Favorite Folktales & Fabulous Fables | 10.95 | |
| | | | | | Super Science | 10.95 | |
| | | | | | It All Adds Up! | 9.95 | |
| | | | | | History Is A Story Well Told | 9.95 | |
| | | | | | Good Enough To Eat! | 9.95 | |
| | | | | | Welcome, Spring! | 9.95 | |
| | | | | | Animals! Animals! Animals! | 9.95 | |
| | | | | | Learning With Literature | 9.95 | |
| | | | | | | | |

BOOKS NOT IMMEDIATELY AVAILABLE WILL BE PLACED ON 'BACK ORDER AND SHIPPED WHEN RECEIVED, UNLESS OTHERWISE REQUESTED.

| SOLD TO: | SHIP TO: | Subtotal: |
|---|---|---|
| Name | Name | *Sales Tax: |
| Street | Street | Shipping: |
| City | City | TOTAL: |
| State Zip | State Zip | * (WA 8.6%) |
| Daytime Phone ( ) | Purchase Order # | **Shipping & Handling** |
| **METHOD OF PAYMENT:** U.S. funds only | | Under $30.00 ... $4.85 |
| © Check © Visa © Mastercard | Expiration Date: | $30.01 - 60.00 ... $5.85 |
| Card # | Signature: | Over $60.00 ..... $7.85 |

ALLOW 2-3 WEEKS FOR DELIVERY. BOOKS SUBJECT TO STOCK AVAILABILITY AND PRICES SUBJECT TO CHANGE. SCHOOL PURCHASE ORDERS ACCEPTED. →

# ♥ ONE FROM THE HEART - ORDER FORM ♥

| Qty | NEW & *SEASONAL* TITLES | Price | TOTAL |
|---|---|---|---|
| | 75 Creative Ways to Publish | 19.95 | |
| | A Llama in the Family | 3.50 | |
| | Alternatives to Worksheets | 8.95 | |
| | Amanda Pig & Brother Oliver | 3.99 | |
| | Baby In a Basket | 14.99 | |
| | Bal Reading K-2 | 12.95 | |
| | Bal Reading 3-6 | 12.95 | |
| | Beyond the Book | 15.95 | |
| | Big Bad Bruce | 6.95 | |
| | Bravest Cat, The | 3.95 | |
| | Bread, Bread,Bread | 4.95 | |
| | Building Literacy w Interactive Charts | 12.95 | |
| | Bunny Money | 14.95 | |
| | Celebrations | 17.95 | |
| | Charts for Children | 12.95 | |
| | Chibi | 14.95 | |
| | Children Just Like Me | 18.95 | |
| | Chrysanthemum | 4.95 | |
| | Cinderella Penguin | 4.99 | |
| | Classroom Centers | 15.95 | |
| | Clever Letters | 9.95 | |
| | Daily Journals | 9.95 | |
| | Dear Children of the Earth | 11.95 | |
| | Develop Literacy Using Reading | 14.95 | |
| | Family Math | 18.00 | |
| | First Flight - Story Wright Bros/Tom T. | 3.75 | |
| | Flag We Love | 15.95 | |
| | Fortunately | 5.99 | |
| | From One to One Hundred | 5.99 | |
| | Gingerbread Boy | 14.95 | |
| | Gobble Up Math | 10.95 | |
| | Graphic Organizer | 12.95 | |
| | Graphing Across Curriculum | 10.95 | |
| | Hat, The | 16.95 | |
| | House on Maple Street | 4.95 | |
| | How to Make a Book | 10.95 | |
| | I Like Books | 5.99 | |
| | I Like It When | 10.95 | |
| | I Like Me | 4.99 | |
| | I Love You Purplest | 14.95 | |
| | I Took My Frog | 4.99 | |
| | If You're Trying to Teach Kids | 14.95 | |
| | Important Book | 5.95 | |
| | Kids On the Net | 14.95 | |
| | James and the Dinosaurs | 16.00 | |
| | Junie B. Jones Series Books | 3.99 | |
| | Little Gorilla | 5.95 | |
| | M & M Counting | 6.95 | |
| | Mail Myself to You | 2.95 | |
| | Make Cards | 11.99 | |
| | Making Books Across Curriculum | 14.95 | |
| | Martha Speaks | 5.95 | |
| | Math Journals | 16.95 | |
| | Miss Malarkey | 5.95 | |
| | Moon & I | 4.95 | |
| | More Stories to Solve | 4.95 | |
| | Moving on-Spelling | 12.95 | |
| | Mr. Lincoln's Whiskers | 15.95 | |
| | Mrs. Peachtree's Bicycle | 15.00 | |
| | My Crayons Talk | 14.95 | |
| | My Friends | 5.95 | |
| | Nasty, Stinky Sneakers | 4.50 | |
| | Never Babysit the Hippos | 5.95 | |
| | Octopus is Amazing | 4.95 | |
| | One Hundred is a Family | 4.95 | |

| Qty | NEW & *SEASONAL* TITLES | Price | TOTAL |
|---|---|---|---|
| | PK Series -- | | |
| | . How Do I Love You | 4.95 | |
| | . I'm Thankful Each Day | 4.95 | |
| | . Just Open a Book | 4.95 | |
| | . Rainbow of Friends | 4.95 | |
| | . That's What a Friend Is | 4.95 | |
| | Paint the Sky - Poetry | 12.95 | |
| | Phonemic Awareness (CTP) | 12.95 | |
| | Phonemic Awareness Activities (Sch) | 9.95 | |
| | Phonics Anytime | 8.95 | |
| | Phonics That Work | 14.95 | |
| | PV - Three Billy Goats | 5.95 | |
| | PV - Goldilocks & Three Bears | 5.95 | |
| | PV - Henny Penny | 5.95 | |
| | PV - Jack & Bean Stalk | 5.95 | |
| | PV - Little Red Hen | 5.95 | |
| | PV - Tortoise & Hare | 5.95 | |
| | Q is for Duck | 5.95 | |
| | Quilt Block History | 8.95 | |
| | Read Across America | 14.95 | |
| | Read, Draw, Solve | 15.95 | |
| | Read- and Write Workshop | 16.95 | |
| | Reading Strategies that Work | 12.95 | |
| | Stories to Solve | 4.95 | |
| | Still More Stories to Solve | 4.95 | |
| | Story of Money | 6.95 | |
| | Story of Statue of Liberty | 5.95 | |
| | THALER - Cinderella Bigfoot | 2.99 | |
| | THALER - Hanzel & Pretzel | 2.99 | |
| | THALER - Princess & Pea-Ano | 2.99 | |
| | THALER - Schmoe White & 7 Dorfs | 2.99 | |
| | THALER - Librarian from Black Lagoon | 2.99 | |
| | This is the Way We Go to School | 4.99 | |
| | Tomorrow's Alphabet | 16.00 | |
| | What in the World | 9.95 | |
| | What Mommies Do Best | 13.00 | |
| | When I Was Little | 5.95 | |
| | Will We Miss Them | 6.95 | |
| | Wooden Teeth & Jelly Beans | 14.95 | |
| | Words, Words, Words | 12.95 | |
| | | | |
| ***Qty*** | ***♥ Your Special Requests ♥*** | | ***TOTAL*** |

See other side for Order information →